MARY ACCORDING TO WOMEN

MARY ACCORDING TO WOMEN

Carol Frances Jegen, BVM
Editor

LEAVEN PRESS

Library of Congress Catalog Card Number:

ISBN: 0-934134-31-6

Published by: Leaven Press
P.O. Box 40292
Kansas City, MO 64141

Printed and bound in the United States of America

Para 7.95 / July 86

Contents

Dedication

To all BVM Sisters
past, present, and to come
especially Maureen D. Cleary
whose overwhelming love for Mary
inspirited the entire Mary Festival

Introduction

In the post-Vatican II years devotion to Mary has received a decidedly different emphasis from that of the years immediately preceding the council. Some people consider this period one of de-emphasis on Mary, almost to the point of silence. Others see our time as one of necessary quiet to offset a somewhat triumphalistic over-emphasis on Mary in popular piety in the pre-Vatican II years. Regardless of one's opinion on this question of recent Marian emphasis, the fact remains that very little has been done to draw out the implications of the particular emphasis Vatican II gave in its statement on Mary in the midst of the church. Furthermore, the worldwide awakening of the equal dignity and role of women in human history gives a certain urgency to a vitalized faith-understanding of Mary for contemporary times. These reasons and others seem to indicate the time has come to probe anew the meaning of our Marian heritage as Catholics who live in the United States of America, a country whose patroness is Mary Immaculate.

By deliberate design, Vatican II began on October 11, then the feast of the Motherhood of Mary, in commemoration of the conciliar proclamation of Mary as Mother of God in AD 431 at Ephesus. After considerable debate the Second Vatican Council did not give us a separate document on Mary. Rather, the final chapter of the dogmatic constitution on the church, *Lumen Gentium,* focused on "The Role of the Blessed Virgin Mary, Mother of God, in the Mystery of Christ and the Church." This same Ecumenical Council, in its ecclesiological focus, turned the church outward to the world. In the opening statement of the pastoral constitution on the church, *Gaudium et Spes,* often referred to as *The Church in the Modern World,* all Christians were reminded that the "joys and hopes, the griefs and anxieties of the people of this age, especially those who are poor or an any way afflicted" must be the "joys and hopes, the griefs and anxieties of the followers of Christ." From one point of view, the final Marian chapter in *Lumen Gentium* can be considered a link between these two conciliar documents on ecclesiology. That is to say, Vatican II presents Mary actively present in the midst of the renewing church, now more conscious than ever of its mission to the world. The 1983 Mary Festival at Mundelein College in Chicago focused on this Vatican II emphasis on Mary's vital role in today's church discovering new ways to be faithful to its gospel commitment to renew the face of the earth.

The question might be asked as to why such needed theological probing of a contemporary meaning of Mary was developed as a festival. Although "festival" can designate a program of cultural events, it highlights a celebrative aspect to such a program. Festivals are times of rejoicing. The mystery of Mary in our midst is indeed cause for celebration. In a new and perhaps unprecedented way, the Mary of the Second Vatican Council is truly a "cause of our joy," to quote a familiar, well-loved title for Mary in the Litany of Loretto.

Familiar titles for Mary were chosen as the organizing principle around which the entire Mary Festival was developed. "Seat of Wisdom," "Comforter of the Afflicted," "Mirror of Justice"—titles for Mary also taken from her litany, helped situate the Mary Festival in the long tradition of Marian devotion in the church. The use of such familiar titles witnessed to the transitional motif so prominent in all of Vatican II in its efforts to be faithful to the age-old tradition of the church as the council projected that same church into a very new and uncharted future. The seven Marian titles developed in the Mary Festival were selected because of their particular resonance with contemporary issues, especially as those issues have been addressed since the Second Vatican Council by women in new ministerial roles.

The theology symposium of Mundelein's Mary Festival was enhanced by special pastoral sessions on Mary in Prayer, Mary in Education, and Mary in Media. Book and art displays, colorful banners for each title of Mary, an artistic presentation of Marian music and art—all added an indispensable festive character. Processions, evensong, eucharistic celebrations, and an agape picnic made a contemporary theology of Mary vibrant with the joy and excitement that belong by right to the proclamation of God's good news.

The papers comprising the theology symposium are presented in this book. The seven authors experienced a community research effort as they shared outlines and drafts and bibliographical suggestions. In the actual presentation of the final rendition of each paper during the Mary Festival, the intrinsic unity of the entire project became more apparent than ever. Wholehearted, enthusiastic audience response attested to a vital theology of Mary people can make their own today.

Throughout these essays, the question of symbolization arises with respect to Mary. Each author is concerned with finding new meanings in the Mary symbols that are deeply rooted in Christian consciousness. Without losing the positive values of personal compassion and caring traditionally evoked by the image of Mary, a continual effort is made to relate Mary's compassionate concern to the societal order. Such transference of meaning is not meant to be a substitute of social involvement for personal solicitude, but rather an harmonious blending of the gospel imperative of love in its demands for action on behalf of justice and peacemaking. The psychological implications of such symbolic transfer are great and merit study all on their own. Perhaps this volume can serve as a catalyst in that direction.

The Mary Festival was planned as part of the 150th Jubilee Celebration of the Sisters of Charity of the Blessed Virgin Mary, the congregation that founded Mundelein College for women more than fifty years ago. It was especially appropriate that this college, whose theologians were the first women to design, inaugurate, direct, and staff a graduate program in religious studies, should also be the first college whose women presented and celebrated a Mary Festival. Susan Rink, BVM, then president of Mundelein, gave her wholehearted support and encouragement. To her and to each BVM sister whose spirit and cooperation made the Mary Festival possible, our gratitude is endless. Special gratitude is due to Rose Barry, BVM, for her care in typing the manuscript, and to Montylou Wilson for her invaluable editorial services.

Carol Frances Jegen, BVM

Nativity of Mary
September 8, 1983

BIOGRAPHICAL DATA

Ann Carr, BVM (Ph.D. University of Chicago) Associate Professor of Theology, University of Chicago Divinity School.

Mary De Cock, BVM (M.A. Marquette University; M.A. University of Chicago) Associate Professor of Religious Studies, Mundelein College.

Mary Donahey, BVM (Ph.D. Columbia University and Union Theological Seminary) Associate Professor of Religious Studies, Mundelein College.

Margaret I. Healy, BVM (Ph.D. University of Minnesota) Professor of Education; Director of Government Relations, Mundelein College.

Carol Frances Jegen, BVM (Ph.D. Marquette University) Professor of Religious Studies, Mundelein College.

Mary Lauranne Lifka, BVM (Ph.D. University of Michigan) Associate Professor of History, St. Teresa's College, Winona, MN.

Rose Marie Lorentzen, BVM (M.A. Mundelein College; M.Div. Jesuit School of Theology, Chicago) Pastoral Minister, Diocese of Rockford.

MARY IN THE MYSTERY OF THE CHURCH: VATICAN COUNCIL II
Anne Carr, BVM

Contemporary Interpretations of Mary

A 1982 newspaper article headlined "Woman Quits in Virgin Mary Fuss" reported that the leader of a Catholic women's organization in West Germany aroused a storm of protest when she claimed that "the traditional image of the Virgin Mary contributes to sexual frustration in German marriages." The woman resigned her post because of the controversy following a televised discussion program in which she questioned the virtues historically ascribed to Mary by the church. "The picture of Mary as 'an example of purity, chastity, and virginity' is inaccurate," she said. It contributes to tensions and breakdowns in marriage "when Catholic women try to reconcile their sexual behavior in marriage with the model of abstinence embodied by the Virgin Mary." Further, she objected to the "traditional image of Mary as a 'meek and submissive' woman" when in reality she must have been an "active, self-assured, plucky woman . . . rational, questioning, able to debate."[1]

About the same time, an article by Mary Gordon, author of *Final Payments* and *The Company of Women,* elaborated on the problem Mary is for Catholic women. "In my high school days," she wrote, "Mary was a stick to beat smart girls with. Her example was held up constantly: an example of silence, of subordination, of the pleasure of taking the back seat.

> For women like me, it was necessary to reject that image of Mary in order to hold onto the fragile hope of intellectual achievement, independence of identity, sexual fulfillment.

Yet we were offered no alternative to this Marian image;
hence we were denied a potent female image whose appli-
cation was universal. There were a few saints one could, in
desperation, turn to: Teresa of Avila, who was reported to
have a fresh mouth ('If this is the way you treat your friends,
Lord, what do you do to your enemies?' Henny Youngman
in Carmel. Who wouldn't like her?), talked back to bishops,
reformed her order, had visions whose power and authen-
ticity were unassailable. But any saint, however celebrated,
is venerated out of choice, only by some. The appeal of Mary
is that devotion to her is universal, ancient. And she is the
Mother of God."[2]

Gordon notes that, with the emergence of the feminist movement,
some women rejected Mary in favor of her son, but that now sophisticated female thought is attempting to retrieve the history of women, to
search for the female past that is often anonymous and uncredited. "To
look for new values that are not simply male values dressed for success
. . . is leading women back to Mary."[3]

But this is problematic, since most of what Christian history tells us
about Mary is seen through men's eyes—the misogynist eyes of the
Fathers of the Church, for example, who exhibit an aversion to female
sexuality and who set Mary apart from the rest of her sex. "She was only
acceptable because she did not share the corruption that was inevitably
attached to the female condition." In a favorite patristic image, Mary
was set against Eve, the symbol of flesh, sin, and evil who was cursed to
bear children; Mary is the happy or blessed virgin, opposite to Eve in
her purity. And women generally were identified with Eve. Chrysostom
writes, e.g., "If you consider what is stored up behind those lovely eyes
[of woman] . . . you will agree [that she] . . . is merely a whitened
sepulcher." For Gordon, it is difficult to understand the horror and
disgust of the Fathers for the physical nature of women symbolized by
Eve, and their veneration for the Virgin Mary.

Studying the Eve/Mary relationship in the patristic literature,
Rosemary Ruether shows that the Fathers believed that only in ascetic
virginity could woman transcend her sinful and corrupt female nature
—symbol of the flesh as evil—and become like a man—symbol of the
spirit. The emergence of Mariology, in the fourth-century writings of

the Fathers with their praise of Mary as the epitome of spiritual womanhood, does not prevent their despising "all real physical women, sex, and fecundity and wholly etherealizing women into incorporeal phantasms in order to provide love objects for the sublimated libido and guard against turning back to any physical expression of love with the dangerous daughters of Eve."[4]

Thus the recovery of Mary for contemporary women must include awareness that her place, as a religious symbol, is part of the history of human thought (mostly male thought) about women, "a history of errors" as Gordon says, that is not unique to Christianity. She calls for a "forgiving vigilance."

> One must forgive, or one must give up history; one must be vigilant to ensure that the tendencies [to denigrate women] so inbred in all human beings—ourselves as well as men— are passed on as little as possible. For they are in all of us, blood and bone; we cannot expect them to disappear in a lifetime. Those of us whose hearts are moved by those who have gone before us, who wish to keep the connection alive, must reject the temptation of historical romanticism. We must not forget the history of woman has been a history of degradation, oppression, the idealization whose other side is tyranny. But we must resist as well the temptation to reject the lonely, the exalted, the resonant life built up for centuries by living men and women.[5]

Gordon's "forgiving vigilance" is not shared by another contemporary feminist writer who has studied the powerful symbol of the Virgin and its effects on the lives of women. Marina Warner's detailed historical treatment of Marian myth, cult, devotion, art, and symbol, concludes that Mary represents, not religious paradox, but ideology. "The Catholic religion . . . binds its female followers . . . on a double wheel." Mary is the symbol of the ideal woman, translated into a moral exhortation that, on the one hand, extols motherhood as the fulfillment of woman's purpose and, on the other, asserts, in the words of the Council of Trent, that "virginity and celibacy are better and more blessed than the bond of matrimony." Since Mary represents an impossible ideal, Warner believes, "the Virgin will recede into legend. . .;

the legend will endure in its splendour and lyricism, but it will be emptied of moral significance. . . ."[6]

Mary Daly, for all her rage against Christianity, offers an analysis of Mary that is more subtle. She notes the autonomous power of Mary's image, discovered, for example, by Henry Adams. Traveling in Europe at the turn of the century, he noticed that the great cathedrals were not dedicated to God, but to Mary:

> Symbol of energy, the Virgin had acted as the greatest force
> the Western world ever felt, and had drawn men's activities
> to herself more strongly than any power, natural or super-
> natural, had ever done.[7]

Daly does not believe there is any demonstrable connection between the Mary symbol and the historical mother of Jesus, but that the power of her image, its "sometimes God-like status," may really be a "fore-telling image, pointing to the future becoming of women 'to the image of God.' " On the surface, according to Daly, Mary by her inimitability functions in Catholicism to put all ordinary women in a caste with the sinful Eve and to reinforce sexual caste with the message that women are holy only in relation to men. Beneath the surface, however, there are prophetic sub-intended meanings in the image of Mary that point to the independence of women. The doctrine of the virgin birth (Mary's virginity before, during, and after the birth of Jesus) indicates that "the woman who is defined as a virgin is not defined exclusively by her relationships with men"; virginity can be a symbol of female autonomy when sifted out of its patriarchal setting as "the vision of the free and independent woman who stands alone."[8]

While for Daly the power of the Mary symbol has been co-opted by men in order to domesticate, cloister, and subordinate the power of women, the doctrines of the Immaculate Conception and the Assumption can also be read for their unintended, or double, meanings. Thomas Aquinas and many other theologians rejected the Immaculate Conception because Mary's exemption from original sin seemed to detract from the dignity of Christ and his redemption. When the dogma was promulgated in 1854, the resistance of some Catholics and the shock of Protestants, writes Daly, "indicate that they dimly glimpsed the un-intended threat to male supremacy" in the affirmation of Mary's singularity in freedom from original sin. The Assumption of Mary was hailed by psychologist Carl Jung because it symbolizes Mary as the "fourth person" of the Trinity, raising the feminine (often projected as a symbol of evil) to the level of the divine. While Daly knows this specific meaning would never be accepted by the church, she believes that the fulness of the Mary symbol bears important prophetic possibility for women.

Other contemporary writers also see prophetic possibilities in the symbol of Mary. Rosemary R. Ruether interprets Mary, the mother of Jesus, and the other Marys of the New Testament, Jesus' disciples and friends, as representing the "feminine face of the church." Placed in a context of authentic reciprocity, the balance of activity and receptivity in the fully human person (no longer stereotyped as male and female) might be fostered by a new appreciation of Mary in the church. If the symbols of Christ and Mary can be freed from models of male dominance and female passivity, a humanizing of the church might occur in which "Christ represents the emptying out of a divine power . . . at the service of others and Mary, or the church, represents liberated humanity."[9] Andrew M. Greeley believes that the centuries of Marian symbolism—madonna, virgo, sponsa, pieta—reflect the femininity of God and respond to important human and religious experiences.[10] Elisabeth Schüssler Fiorenza holds that Catholicism's traditional devotion to Mary is significant because of the central place of a woman in its religious horizon. As the figure of Jesus became more transcendent and divinized, Mary expressed the qualities of tenderness, compassion, and mercy of the biblical God. And as the figure of Mary became more transcendent and divinized in Catholic devotional life, she reflected the feminine side of God, of Christ, and of the church.[11]

This overview of contemporary interpretations of Mary—both negative and positive—may set the stage for our discussion of Mary in the mystery of the church, as she is described by the Second Vatican Council. These interpretations alert us to the power of the symbol of Mary, a religious symbol that, as Rahner and Tillich have shown, opens us to participation in the very mystery to which it points.[12] They warn us to be vigilant in our interpretations of Mary, to be watchful of the way a symbol can be used, its positive and negative effects on the lives of people. No symbol in itself is simply oppressive or liberating: its uses, whether religious, political or social, must be considered as we discover

its effects on the lives of people and as we offer new interpretations. For
it is new interpretations, in dialog with tradition and with contemporary questions, and not mere repetition that make tradition a living and
always new truth—authentic revelation.[13] And as Paul Ricoeur has
demonstrated, new interpretation of the multi-valent levels of a symbol in its excess of meaning must include both suspicion and restoration
—suspicion of its regressive possibilities, restoration of its progressive
meanings.[14] The doctrine, image, and symbol of Mary have had both
negative and positive import, especially for women in the church.
What, then, are the effects of the teaching about Mary of the Second
Vatican Council?

Vatican II: Historical Background

Chapter 8 of the *Dogmatic Constitution on the Church (Lumen
Gentium)*, "The Role of the Blessed Virgin Mary, Mother of God, in the
Mystery of Christ and the Church," presents material for an intriguing
historical study. From the preparatory phase in 1962 until the promul-
gation of the finally approved text on November 21, 1964, the document went through some sixteen revisions.[15] "The decision to include
the chapter on the Blessed Virgin Mary in *this* Constitution (instead of
in a separate schema) was the closest of all votes taken in St. Peter's."[16]
Clearly, Mary was a controversial issue at the Second Vatican Council.
Why was she the source of such extended debate and eventual compromise? In the language used at the time, so-called "maximalist" and
"minimalist" positions on Mary were held by opposing groups among
the Fathers of the Council and their theologian advisers. These catch
phrases came to bear an extra burden of meaning: one who was
"maximalist" was understood to be less theologically rigorous, especially in favoring a separate council document devoted to Mary alone
that, from the side of the opponents, represented a detachment of the
discussion of Mariology—a certain independence—from the rest of
theology. One who was a "minimalist," on the other hand, could be
reproached for having little love for Mary, of being so ecumenically
sensitive to the feelings of Protestants (disturbed by what appeared to
be near equation of Mary with Jesus Christ) that they were willing to

sacrifice Catholic doctrine for the cause of church union. "Should we give in," wrote one commentator, "to the impulse to enrich the glorious titles of the Mother of God, or should we maintain a safer exposition of her role in the plan of salvation, safeguarding thus the homogeneity of theology as a whole?"[17]

Thus Mary, and the question of a special separate text devoted to her place in Catholic life, became an emotionally charged issue among the bishops at the council during its second session in the autumn of 1963. On the one side, Cardinal Henriquez of Chile, speaking for some 44 Latin American bishops, requested on October 1 that the text on Mary be included in the document on the church, pointing out that in Latin America, devotion to Mary is sometimes too isolated from the central devotional life of the church. Several days later, a Spanish bishop, representing 66, mostly Spanish, bishops, spoke against the inclusion of the text in the church document "because the mystery of Mary is greater than the mystery of the church."[18] The issue was drawn, interestingly enough, between Latin bishops on either side of the Atlantic, the old world and the new.

While the theological commission of the council had itself voted, by a two-thirds majority, for inclusion of the text on Mary in the church document, it decided to ask for a general vote on the question from the council fathers. The commission named Cardinal Santos of Manila to speak for a separate text and Cardinal Koenig of Vienna to speak for inclusion. Santos argued that the text on the church was too short to allow for inclusion of the schema on Mary "without her dignity and place in the church thereby suffering. . . ," that "Mariology should not be reduced to ecclesiology." Koenig argued that the church was the central topic of the council and that "a separate schema would give the impression that new dogmas are being proposed"; that the present trend in theology was to link Mary and the church, using both scriptural and patristic sources, in a way that both Protestant and Eastern Christians find more acceptable. Five days later the vote would be taken. There was real fear that this issue might split the council. Five different documents on Mary were being circulated, and implications of heresy—for example, denial by omission of the doctrines of the Immaculate Conception and the Assumption—began to appear in the press, as well as vicious accusations that equated inclusion with all that was evil and dangerous in so-called "progress" (*progressimo*). Michael Novak reported that the week before the vote on Mary was taken was "the blackest . . . of the council," that "the winds of forward motion had dropped, and storms were forming in the dark."[19]

Novak's analysis, "Politics and the Blessed Virgin Mary," written during the second session of the council, offered an interpretation of Mary as the key symbol in the conciliar struggle between "non-historical orthodoxy" and Pope John's vision of an "open church." He described non-historical orthodoxy as an other-worldly piety that "seems more pagan than Christian," that ignores the social and political implications of the gospel in separating personal devotion from public life. He wrote:

> Non-historical orthodoxy is essentially masochistic. The prophecy of imminent doom is its *raison d'etre*. It needs to feel attacked. It needs to profess the very items of its belief most calculated to arouse the ire of non-Catholics, in order to have the assurance that the world is still at war with it . . . . (It) is a retreat from the responsibilities of living in history, and of remaining faithful to Christ under the stresses of changing circumstance.[20]

Within the piety of non-historical orthodoxy, Novak argued, "popular devotions, especially Marian devotions, loom very large" because they "are ordinarily a refuge from the conflicts of history." To a focus on Mary—symbolized in the council by a separate schema for her—Novak linked withdrawal from the problems of the world, focus on personal sins or misdemeanors, intellectual ignorance of the biblical and liturgical foundations of Christianity, fear of change, and anti-communism. This spirituality was especially prevalent in Spain and Italy, he wrote, countries that had not experienced social revolutions, whose class structures remained rigid, and whose political power groups have a great stake in keeping "the energy of the church involved in private devotions to Mary and the saints."[21]

On the other hand, those who urged the inclusion of the text on Mary in the document on the church represented "Catholic scholars who labored at a theology of the Word of God, of the liturgy, of social action, of the return to the earlier traditions of Christianity." They represented, in the council, the forces for genuine renewal, the open church of creativity and historical fidelity to God's word, and to the church's intellectual tradition, in short, the activity of the Spirit. When the important and symbolic vote was taken on October 30, the council voted for inclusion of the Mary text in the Constitution on the Church by a vote of 1,114 to 1,074, the small margin of 40 votes demonstrating a fundamental and potentially serious split in the historic gathering.[22] Nevertheless, the closest vote of the entire council went with the forces for change.

Before we turn to the text on Mary that was included in *Lumen Gentium,* we might well ponder a bit, from the perspective of 20 more years and the varied interpretations of Mary with which we began, what might have been at stake for women in the fiercely emotional conciliar debate about Mary. Novak is again an instructive contemporary source. In his discussion of the other-worldly Marian piety of non-historical orthodoxy, he wrote:

> The man of history has little time for such devotions, such attitudes. This form of piety attempts to womanize the world, according to the spirit of an earlier century. In effect, it insists that men withdraw from the real, concrete daily work of human progress. Not by accident does non-historical orthodoxy have a stronger hold on women than on men, especially in the lower classes; these are the ones whose lives have changed least since the late Middle Ages.[23]

Novak also reported that on the morning of the vote, journalists were invited to attend the council Mass. Some 20 did so, and as they went forward to receive communion, a male functionary motioned to the one woman journalist, Eva Fleischner, that she should stop. As she moved ahead, the man gestured violently, then physically prevented her from approaching the communion rail. On the next occasion when journalists were invited to the council Mass, "women were expressly excluded."[24] In what way, we will ask next, was another woman, Mary, included at Vatican II?

Role of the Blessed Virgin in the Economy of Salvation

Commentators on the council point out that all of its documents were honed through debate over different points of view, but that a few texts were debated with particular intensity: the text on Mary was one of these.[25] At issue were a variety of Mariological themes put forward by different schools and thinkers. One was the question of a fundamental principle of Mariology, in which theologians sought for a single, unifying center from which everything significant about Mary could be deduced. Another was the question of whether Mary should be discussed in a "Christo-typical" or an "ecclesio-typical" focus. Yet another was whether emphasis should be on Mary's function or her privileges—function stressing her closeness to human beings, privilege stressing her closeness to God. [26] Because of the variety of technical themes, in addition to the diversity of popular piety with its various local expression, the impression was often given of fundamental disagreement throughout the debates. Nevertheless, after 16 drafts, the final text was finally produced and approved.

The first and central theme one notices is that Mary is placed within the wider framework of the whole economy of salvation. Where the concern had been expressed, especially from Latin America, that Marian devotion was tending to become isolated and detached from the central life of the church, in *Lumen Gentium* Mary is integrated into the whole of Catholic theology, in clear relationship *both* to Christ and to the church. The chapter boldly cites I Timothy 2:5-6: "For there is one God, and one Mediator between God and men, himself, man, Christ Jesus, who gave himself a ransom for all." Immediately after the first citation, it adds:

> The maternal duty of Mary toward men in no way obscures
> or diminishes this unique mediation of Christ, but rather
> shows its power. For all the saving influences of the Blessed
> Virgin on men originate, not from some inner necessity,
> but from the divine pleasure. They flow forth from the
> super-abundance of the merits of Christ, rest on His media-
> tion, depend entirely on it, and draw all their power from it.
> In no way do they impede the immediate union of the
> faithful with Christ. Rather, they foster this union.[27]

This remarkable passage is stong in its assertion that Mary is not to be understood in isolation but rather in relation to God and to Christ. It follows a preface that relates Mary to the mystery of salvation and a long section in which Mary's role is described in biblical terms: in a traditional interpretation of Old Testament prophecies, with a focus on Mary's active consent to God's saving initiative in Christ, "in subordination to Him and along with Him, by the grace of Almighty God she served the mystery of redemption."[28] Traces of Mary in the New Testament are cited in which she is described in her special position but always in relation to Jesus. And there is clear reaffirmation of the dogmas of the Immaculate Conception and the Assumption.[29]

What is significant about these opening sections of the chapter on Mary is the inclusion, in brief space, of all the controversial issues: Mary is subordinated to God and to Christ, yet she is elevated in the plan of salvation. She is described in biblical terms, yet in readings that include traditional especially patristic exegesis. She is clearly placed in relationship to the fundamental mystery of the church, and yet the church's later dogmas about her special character are reaffirmed. Compromise worked to produce "a balanced text," in the eyes of many Catholics, but an "uneasy juxtaposition of salvation history and dogma," according to one Protestant commentator.[30]

There is important ecumenical significance in the diminishment of what were called "Marian excesses," by the document's sober restraint in placing Mary in auxiliary relationship to Jesus Christ. Thus might be allayed Protestant Christians' fears about Catholic tendencies to divinize Mary, especially in the nineteenth and twentieth centuries, in the statements of Pius IX, X, XI, and XII, and so to remove her from salvation in Christ alone. There is a minimum number of citations of papal pronouncements and an abundance of biblical and patristic references, especially from the Greek fathers, thus recognizing Eastern Christianity's ancient and continuing devotion to Mary as the Mother of God. Yet nothing truly Catholic is left out: the dogmas of the Immaculate Conception and the Assumption are affirmed and devotion to Mary is encouraged.[31]

More than ecumenical concern, however, lay behind placing Mary in relationship to the centrality of Jesus Christ. The pastoral character of Vatican II meant that it was concerned to provide orientation for Catholics within the church. Placing Mary within the wider economy of salvation in Christ by affirming her redemption in Christ, Christ's unique work of salvation, and the direct union of Christians with Christ was meant to restore the harmony of Catholic devotional practice within the church's liturgical and sacramental life. Where Marian devotions—the rosary, various novenas, for example—had come to be placed on a par with (or even as more important than) the Eucharist and the other sacraments, the intent and effect of the conciliar treatment were to place Mary and devotions to her in relation to Christ and the Eucharist.

Yet one today may question the effect of this move to subordinate Mary in relation to Christ, especially as she represents the figure of the woman in the church. Was the effect—intentional or not—also to diminish her importance in some absolute sense and so to diminish the importance of the female in the church? Was the intention—conscious or not—using Novak's words, to de-womanize the church? It is a complex issue, as we look back from the vantage point of the contemporary women's movement in the church and its impetus to restore the powerful and prophetic aspects of Mary in contemporary life. Before attempting to answer that difficult question, we should examine a second central theme in Second Vatican Council's treatment of Mary: the discussion of her as Mother of the Church. Was this a new title for Mary?

Mary, Mother of the Church and the Cult of the Virgin

The title *Mater Ecclesiae* is not in fact explicitly used in the chapter on Mary in *Lumen Gentium*, although it is implied in several passages. It is foreshadowed in the earlier section on sciptural evidences of Mary in the life of Jesus, especially the stories of Cana and Calvary in the gospel of John. The Calvary account vividly suggests her maternal relationship to the church:

> Thus the Blessed Virgin advanced in her pilgrimage of faith, and loyally persevered in her union with her Son unto the cross. There she stood, in keeping with the divine plan (cf. John 19:25), suffering grievously with her only begotten Son. There she united herself with a maternal heart to His sacrifice, and lovingly consented to the immolation of this Victim which she herself had brought forth. Finally, the same Christ Jesus dying on the cross gave her as a mother to

his disciple. This he did when He said: "Woman, behold thy son" (John 19:26-27).[32]

The inclusion of the chapter on Mary of course indicates at once that she is to be seen in reference to the mystery of the church. Mary is a type of the church itself and exercises a maternal role within the church. Typologically, she represents the perfection of the church as the model of faith, hope, and love—the perfect disciple, as theologians are saying today—and in her Assumption, a sign of the future fulfillment of the church.[33] Mary also exercises an active, maternal function within the church toward all its members. The *Constitution* links Mary's eternal predestination to be the Mother of God with her active faith at the Annunciation and her faith beneath the cross. "In an utterly singular way she cooperated by her obedience, faith, hope, and burning charity in the Savior's work of restoring supernatural life to souls. For this reason she is a mother to us in the order of grace."[34] What does this motherhood mean?

According to the text, it consists in "the influence Mary exercises on the attainment of the new life" to which Christians are called. This influence is twofold in character. On the one hand, her power is shown in her motherhood of Christ, both as a physical reality and as her reception of God's word (at the Annunciation) in faith. On the other hand, her motherhood continues "without interruption" until the end of history because she continues to win eternal salvation for us by her "manifold acts of intercession." This particularly active role of Mary is dependent on the overflowing abundance of Christ's salvation and receives all its power from his mediation. The council goes no further in describing this influence and intercession. What are we to make of this? At least this much: that in its most recent authoritative and ecumenical gathering, the church speaks of the "maternal charity" of Mary for the "brethren" (and, one may hope, the sisters) of Christ who "journey on earth surrounded by dangers and difficulties until they are led to their happy fatherland." The sexist language of 20 years ago is disturbing today, but the amazing thing is Catholicism's affirmation that a woman, Mary, is an authentically religious figure on our spiritual horizon, and that the titles of Advocate (usually reserved to the Holy Spirit), Auxiliatrix, Adjutrix and Mediatrix are reaffirmed, understood of course in relation to "the dignity and efficacy of Christ the one Mediator." The more controversial title, Coredemptrix, is not used at all. An analogy is suggested about the relation of Mary to Christ in the way that the ordained priesthood and the priesthood of the faithful are related to the priesthood of Christ, which "does not exclude but rather gives rise among creatures to a manifold cooperation which is but a sharing in this unique source."[35] Mary is to Christ as human priesthood (both ordained and lay) is to Christ's priesthood. Thus she is firmly placed on the human side of the divine/human relationship.

Like Mary, the church itself is understood as both virgin and mother, a powerful patristic theme. The council draws on the traditional Eve/Mary symbolism in several places to highlight Mary's active faith and obedience. Eve and Mary are contrasted in terms of disobedience and obedience, unbelief and faith, death and life: Mary is "the new Eve, who put her absolute trust not in the ancient serpent but in God's messenger." It is for this reason that Mary brought forth Christ as the firstborn of many faithful: "In their birth and development she cooperates with a maternal love." The church, like Mary, is a mother in accepting God's word, bears children by its preaching and baptism, children who are "born of God." The church is also a virgin in fidelity to Christ; in the purity of its faith, hope, and love it becomes more like its exalted model in the search for holiness and apostolic mission.[36]

This ecclesial framework is carried over in the way Christians approach Mary: "The council insists on the pre-eminence of the liturgical cult of Mary, which again accentuates her relationship to Christ and the Trinity . . . without interfering with traditional extra-liturgical devotions."[37] Mary's significance is her special relation to the mysteries of Christ: This is the source of ancient devotion to her as "God-bearer," the one to whom Christians have turned for protection. Thus she is the object of devotion, and such devotion should be encouraged in the church, though always with awareness of its distinction from the adoration that is due to Christ and to the Father and the Holy Spirit. Exaggeration and narrowmindedness, emotionalism and credulity are to be avoided, as well as anything that might be misinterpreted by non-Catholic Christians. Mary's cult is meant to lead to faith; through love for her as a mother we are to imitate her virtues.[38]

Thus Mary's motherhood is related to the mystery of the church and devotion to her is to be integrated in liturgical and apostolic life. The title *Mater Ecclesiae,* controversial because of ecumenical concerns, was eventually proclaimed by Pope Paul VI, in November, 1964, the same day that *Lumen Gentium* was promulgated. Mary is "mother of the church, of the whole Christian people, both of the faithful and of pastors." This declaration makes it clear that Mary's motherhood is of persons and not of the institutional elements of the church; it is a motherhood in the realm of personal grace.[39] Mary is the model of spiritual receptivity to God's grace, not of hierarchial power.[40]

This spiritual focus is confirmed when the text describes her as summoning "the faithful to her Son and His sacrifice, and to love for the Father." The church is to seek after the glory of Christ and so to become like Mary, its model, in continual growth in faith, hope, and love, "searching out and doing the will of God in all things." Thus Mary is also the model of the church in its apostolic work: as she brought forth Christ, the church's work is the birth of Christ in the hearts of the faithful; her maternal love should animate all who participate in the mission of the church.[41]

Mary as Sign of Hope for the Pilgrim Church

The final brief section of the chapter on Mary recapitulates the theme already apparent in earlier parts, of her bodily and spiritual glory in heaven, not as removed from our lives but as continuing "in this present world as the image and first flowering of the church as she is to be perfected in the world to come." Emphasizing the unity of Mary's bodily and spiritual glory in heaven, the council affirms the central Christian idea of the resurrection of the body, the flesh as the sacrament of human spiritual life. In her Assumption, Mary is a sign of the church's final hope and a comfort to God's pilgrim people. Christians are urged to pray that Mary as "the Mother of God and of men" intercede with Christ, as she did at the beginnings of the church, "until all the peoples of the human family," whether Christians or not, "are happily gathered into the one People of God for the glory of the Most Holy . . . Trinity."[42]

In this short section, the major themes of the whole document on the church are drawn together—the church as the people of God on pilgrimage in the solidarity of the whole human community, the final goal of the human journey in the life of the triune God. And "by anticipation Mary stands out alone as the perfect church, the perfected community of the faithful."[43] In a century that has experienced terrible wars, massive destruction of human life and of centers of civilization (one thinks of the Jewish Holocaust, the fire-bombing of Dresden, the bombs dropped on Hiroshima and Nagasaki, and our current situation of nuclear threat), there is affirmation of the final dignity and exaltation of the human body. In a time in which a widespread philosophy emerged of the meaninglessness and absurdity of life, of human existence as a being-toward-death in final nothingness, the Catholic Church affirmed that in a *woman*, the Mother of God, ultimate meaning for the whole of the human, matter and spirit, is already realized.

Finally, the council expresses joy and comfort in the devotion to Mary as virgin and mother of Eastern Christians, of some separated Christians, and implores her intercession "in the fellowship of all the saints," "until all the people of the human family," whether Christian or not, are "gathered together in peace and harmony into the one People of God" for God's glory.[44] Mary is thus seen as a symbol of a human community united in peace and harmony. A woman is the sign of a humankind fully transformed.

Reflections on the Significance of Vatican II and Mary

The major import of the chapter on Mary in the *Constitution on the Church* can be seen in its effects both outside and inside the Catholic Church. Outside, the brief and restrained document served to allay Protestant fears about the Marian excesses of Catholics. The text placed Mary in a biblical and traditional context as a special figure, but one who was clearly on the human side of the divine/human relationship. Her special or privileged character lies in her significance not only as mother of God but as mother of the church. As such she is clearly human, not divine. She is herself redeemed by Christ and her maternal role in our lives is entirely dependent on Christ, relative to his work of redemption. Though Mary is special in God's plan of salvation, it is her faith, hope, and love that warrant her unique place in the devotional life of the church. That devotion is fostered and encouraged, but always in relationship to worship directed toward *God*: Father, Son, and Spirit. The Marian text, placed in the context of the church document and other major texts on revelation and the liturgy, made it clear that Mary was not a rival to Christ or his equal in the economy of salvation. At the same time, the traditional veneration of Mary in Eastern Christianity is reaffirmed in the use of patristic themes—the mother of God, for example—and the sparing use of citations from papal pronouncements of the nineteenth and twentieth centuries.

Inside the church, however, the result was a diminishment of Marian devotion and spirituality. Not simply the brief chapter on Mary, but also the other major themes of the council served to focus attention elsewhere: on biblical and liturgical renewal, on the church as the whole people of God, and on the enormous social questions of the church in relation to the contemporary world. Gradually—or was it overnight?— Mary seemed to disappear from public Catholic consciousness. Rosaries and novenas dropped out of sight in the emphasis on the new vernacular liturgy that inspired a bibically oriented community worship and celebrated salvation in Christ in a trinitarian and eucharistic framework. The recovery of the Bible for Catholics after Vatican II was a momentous event that, not without some pain, loss, and nostalgia, reoriented and integrated the church's liturgical and spiritual life. And in the Bible, Mary plays a rather minor role. The chapter of the church document on Mary uses biblical material, but in the "uneasy juxtaposition of salvation history and dogma" alluded to earlier, and with an interweaving of the patristic Eve/Mary symbolism that stresses Mary's perfection in contrast to Eve's sin. We might examine the use of scriptural material, and the Eve/Mary symbolism, in order to form a critical appraisal of the text from the perspective of 20 years.

Recent biblical scholarship on Mary is quite tempered in comparison with some past theological treatment of her. In Mark's gospel she is described in very human terms as, at one point, standing outside the group of Jesus' followers: "she did not follow Jesus about as a disciple during the ministry."[45] Luke softens this negative picture by affirming that after the death and resurrection of Jesus, Mary "shared the faith in Jesus of the earliest Christian community" (Acts 1:14) and he reads back her later faith to the time of Jesus' conception. "Her faith does not include clear understanding of all these events, yet . . . she seeks to penetrate their meaning."[46] Luke and Matthew both affirm the virginal conception of Jesus and Luke portrays Mary, in the Magnificat, as one favored by God, blessed because of what God has done to her and because of her faith. Luke does not exalt her as daughter of Zion or the Ark of the Covenant but "as the spokeswoman . . . of the *Anawim,* the poor of Israel, with all the connotations of humble obedience to God . . . implied thereby."[47] John's gospel, a major source for the Vatican II text, contrasts Mary's imperfect faith at Cana with the Calvary scene where she becomes "a model of belief and discipleship." Thus the synoptic gospels suggest a pattern of human growth from doubt to faith while John's symbolic treatment of Mary provides an opening for the "process of further Marian symbolizing within the church."[48]

In comparison with the New Testament evidence about the historical Mary in Scripture, it is apparent that the Mary chapter of the *Constitution on the Church,* for all its softening of Marian excesses and its ecumenical sensitivity, still tends to romanticize and idealize her. It presents a totally positive, somewhat ethereal view of the woman who, in the gospels, is fully human in the growth of her faith—a growth from doubt to belief—as she pondered the meaning of the events surrounding Jesus' birth, ministry, death and resurrection. The chapter introduces dogmatic themes of the Immaculate Conception and the Assumption into the biblical material in a way that conflates scriptural testimony and later, nineteenth- and twentieth-century dogmatic development. The human, historical character of Mary's life tends to disappear in the symbols of her perfection.

Yet in placing the fundamental meaning of Mary within the context of the church, in stressing her faith and her redemption in Christ, the council did not stray far from the biblical picture. Pope Paul VI's declaration of Mary as "Mother of the Church," picking up the main conciliar theme, chose an apt symbol in relation to the biblical material. If the immediate effect of the council was a diminishment of Marian devotions and sentimental tendencies, its long-term result allowed for a more balanced retrieval of Mary in contemporary interpretations. For Mary remains a powerful symbol in the Catholic tradition. Centuries of reflection and prayer are bound into her many local, regional, and universal characterizations. The Second Vatican Council's treatment allows for contemporary interpretations that are biblically based, in faithful dialogue with tradition, and theologically sound.

With regard to the Eve/Mary contrast that is interwoven in the text, it is not biblical scholarship but recent feminist criticism that comes to the fore. We have seen some of the effects of the Eve/Mary symbol in the interpretations of Mary with which we began. An expert on Marian theology, Donal Flanagan, summarizes the issue:

> The Eve/Mary comparison is one of the basic themes of the Marian tradition. This has had a double impact. It singled out Mary as the new Woman, the one in whom man could see perfect womanhood embodied. A price had to be paid for this singling out and the price was the identifying of all other women with the first Eve as fickle, unreliable, morally inferior beings in their natural condition. This dichotomization . . . the process by which the male divides woman by projecting two separate and contradictory symbols of her, did not begin with Christianity. Rather, the Christian Marian tradition in due time produced its own dichotomization in Eve/Mary terms. This allowed the Christian male to project all his respect, honour, love onto one ideal, other-worldly woman, Mary, and thereby to salve his conscience for the actual subjection and low estate he allowed to real women in his patriarchal male-dominated world. We can see here a certain deep and negative element in the Marian tradition. The exalted place accorded to Mary here is accorded in some degree at the expense of womankind. To say that Christianity exalted woman in Mary is true, but it is only telling half the story.[49]

The other half of the story is that history of degradation and oppression to which Mary Gordon referred and in light of which she called for our forgiving vigilance. The Eve/Mary symbolism is adapted from and easily parried with the Adam/Christ symbol of Paul's Epistle to the Romans (5:12-21). But the male pair has seldom been used in the church with such negative effect. Adam has been seen rather as the symbol of human solidarity, a sign of the universality of Christ's redemption. As all have sinned in Adam, all are redeemed in Christ. The Eve/Mary symbol, by contrast, according to recent patristic scholarship, served to identify all real women with Eve while upholding in Mary an impossible ideal (virgin and mother, both terms linked with women's sexuality), an ideal no real woman can fully emulate. As Flanagan suggests, this traditional symbol is the creation of male theologians who have projected both their negative and idealized images of woman onto these symbolic figures.

This symbolism is used in the Vatican II text with precisely the double effect pointed out by both female and male critics. It is used to express Mary's active faith and obedience; she "was used by God not merely in a passive way, but as cooperating in the work of human salvation through free faith and obedience," the council states. Then, quoting Irenaeus, Epiphanius, and Jerome from among the Fathers, " 'The knot of Eve's disobedience was untied by Mary's obedience. What the virgin Eve bound through her unbelief, Mary loosened by her faith.' Comparing Mary with Eve, they call her 'the mother of the living,' and still more often they say: 'Death through Eve, life through Mary.' "[50] On one hand, the text stresses the human activity or agency of Mary—an important aspect for our understanding her as fully human, not merely a passive instrument—and on the other, the disobedience and unbelief of all ordinary women in Eve.

Nevertheless, by placing Mary on the human side of the divine/human relationship in the context of the whole document, she is implicitly placed *with* Eve and with all of us as human, as active recipients of God's redemption in Christ. If recent biblical scholarship has shown the originally imperfect, and gradually growing, faith of Mary—her true humanness—feminist perspectives claim Eve as well as Mary in the solidarity of all human women. There is no need to stigmatize one figure in order to idealize the other. The harmfulness of such dualist thinking—traditional in the Eve/Mary contrast—has been amply shown by feminist thought. It generates a whole series of dichotomies, placing God against or in competition with human beings and the world, humans against and exploitive of the earth, Christ against the church as male over female, husband over wife, spirit over flesh, clergy or religious over laity, etc. If the solidarity of Eve and Mary is affirmed by contemporary women, it is as part of another series of noncompetitive, nondominating modes of relationship projected by feminist theological vision. One does not need to denigrate any part of the human or the earth in order to idealize the other. While women today seek to overcome the images of female inferiority of the past Christian tradition, they are just as concerned to deny any romantic idealization— the pedestal image—in the search for genuine equality and mutuality, a new vision of the integrally human.

It is a misunderstanding on the part of Catholics to believe that the Second Vatican Council and the declaration of Mary as the Mother of the Church meant to diminish the place of Mary in the theological and devotional life of the church. This error was made especially clear by the papal document *Marialis Cultus,* issued by Pope Paul VI in 1974. This text tries to move beyond the submissive, dependent, passive model of Mary entailed in the domestic or conventual portrayal of the recent popes up to Pius XII. It explicitly refers to the changed circumstances of contemporary women in home, politics, employment, social, and cultural contexts. It suggests that the model of Mary as the perfect disciple —one who hears the word of God and acts on it—provides a more biblically based and attractive portrait for today. She is a woman of active and responsible choice. Mary's virginity is as purposeful as her motherhood: availability for God's purpose as it was gradually revealed in the context of her life. Nevertheless one wonders, as Flanagan puts it, if it is enough for the church simply to "preach decisiveness where submissiveness reigned" without explicitly examining the oft-repeated piety that the church's traditional devotion to Mary has always meant honor for women. The Eve/Mary contrast is one illustration among many that this was not the case. [51] There remains such inequality in the church's view of women, much of it rooted in ancient symbolisms which associate women with evil, pollution, sexuality—Eve as the seductive temptress.

Even the contemporary model of Mary as the perfect disciple, whose responsive and active faith is the central significance of both her virginity and her motherhood, can be put in terms that remove her from the experience of ordinary women.[52] The language of perfection, whether applied to the church as the "perfect society" in an older ecclesiology or to the humanity and knowledge of Jesus in an older Christology, is problematic today. The older model of the church as the perfect society has been replaced by contemporary interpretations of the pilgrim church, even a church of sinners, a sinful church that must struggle to respond to God's word in the obscurity and complexity of its ever-changing circumstances.[53] Similarly, the question of Jesus' knowledge has undergone reinterpretation because the idea of perfection which it entails is quite foreign to contemporary Christians, formed as we are by notions of evolution and development. The doctrine of the true humanity of Jesus, according to recent theology, suggests that Jesus' human knowledge was like ours: a gradual coming to awareness of who he was and what his mission demanded, including the possibility of spiritual struggle in a truly human response to God.[54] Likewise, it might be suggested that we need not strain to argue for the perfection of Mary's faith and discipleship from the beginning of her life; rather we can see her as our model in a faith and discipleship that grow and and develop through spiritual struggle in changing circumstance. She is not the superhuman being created by the exaggerations of past, idealizing Mariologies, but the woman of faith who walked in the obscurity and mystery of life much as we do.[55]

In this way she is the mother of the church, an exemplar of human faith, hope, and love, whose full discipleship came to fruition through her own history of trial and suffering, as she faced agonizing difficulties, even as she endured a dark night of faith in the cross of Jesus, her son. Only through her fidelity is she made a sign of our human destiny in the glory of Jesus' resurrection.[56] Contemporary political and liberation theologians argue that Jesus' death was a consequence of his faith, his style of life, his ministry and message; his resurrection was won as a consequence of the pattern of his life and death. A similar pattern can be discerned in Mary's life and in the life of the church for whom she is a model of humankind in service of the kingdom. The Second Vatican Council together with Paul VI's further statements point to her as an examplar of discipleship, of Christian commitment, and as a sign of our destiny as participation in Jesus' resurrection. Today, Christology and ecclesiology "from above," from God's point of view, are rightfully being balanced by focus on the human Jesus and the human church, "from below" in the tangle of human history. So too Mary, mother of Jesus and mother of the church, is seen in her humanness as our sister in faith. She is fully human woman in her receptivity and her agency—demystified, restored to our human history as a sign of an integral and transformed humankind.

Thus she continues to exert her power over the Catholic imagination, especially for women but also for men in new interpretations that emphasize her as the one in whom God does great things, in her identification with the poor of Israel, with the Eves of this world, and with the church's responsive and liberating tasks in this world. Virgin and mother need not be an inimitable ideal, an impossible double bind, but a universal sign of autonomy *and* relationship, strength *and* tenderness, struggle *and* victory, God's power *and* human agency—not in competition but cooperation. She *is* a utopian figure, a mystery, but one who enables us to imagine a healed, reconciled, finally transformed humankind. While it is God who works our salvation in Christ and the Spirit who inspires our active response, it is Mary, a fully human woman, who is the sign of its final completion.

The theology of Mary and her image in the church may ultimately tell us more about the church than about Mary. The theology of Mary may present us with the way the church understands itself and individual Christians, a view always colored by culture and, in this case, by cultural and religious ideas about women. If this is so, then the treatment of Mary in the Second Vatican Council, its focus on her as mother of the church and model of Christian life, witness an important transition in ecclesial self-understanding. It is a transition from an idealized, divinized, absolute model of static perfection—the church as a perfect society that has all truth in advance—to a dynamic image of the earthly, human struggle from unbelief to faith in the ambiguities of history—a pilgrim people in solidarity on their journey toward final transformation in God.

Our historical sketch of the conciliar debate on the chapter on Mary has shown the focus of controversy as a choice between emphasis on Mary's unique privileges, her differences from us, her transcendence or emphasis on her humanness, her likeness to us, her closeness to the church in pilgrimage. The choice to emphasize her as model of the church, her human character as both an historical person of faith and symbol of the church's human journey was and is immensely significant for the church's image of itself. The transition is surely not complete, but an important turn was taken in orientation for a church inclined toward triumphalism, toward claims of perfection here and now.

The issue is important in another way because Mary is also Catholicism's central image of woman. As the church tended toward an unreal idealization of Mary, it tended toward denigration of all other women as Eve and toward the subordination of real women in the church. Thus the ambivalent reaction of thoughtful women today toward the symbol of Mary. Is she a model of subservience, passivity, dependence? Or is she a symbol of prophetic, liberating agency and aut`omony in relation to God and God's realm on earth?

Novak's analysis of the political significance of the conciliar debate in 1963 is a fairly accurate reading of the situation of women and the symbolic status of women in the church at the time. Women did represent the private sphere and its concerns and did symbolize religion as private, personal devotion, removed from the historical and political struggles of society. Recent biblical and theological scholarship had demonstrated the historical, public, and politial significance of Christianity, and thus Novak argued against a womanization of the church in relation to the world, that is, against the church's inward concentration on privatized religion. In so doing, he also witnessed to the cultural and religious appraisal of women—as inferior, backward, privatized. And thus we can see the important small turn registered in the Mary chapter's inclusion in the *Constitution on the Church,* and the major transition of the later *Constitution on the Church in the Modern World (Gaudium et Spes)* to a church facing outward toward the world and its struggles. What Novak missed at the time—or only momentarily glimpsed as he reported the contradiction in barring women journalists from the conciliar masses—was the potentially explosive, indeed subversive, significance of women, popular religion and the lower classes in the church.

The women's movement, in both society and the church, was just beginning to gain momentum in the early 1960s. (The year 1963 saw the publication of Betty Friedan's *The Feminine Mystique,* as well as the conciliar debate on Mary.) Just emerging, too, were other religiously oriented movements for liberation, especially in Latin America, but also in Europe, reflected in the writings of liberation and political theologians with their critiques of Christianity's traditional other-worldliness and their affirmation of popular movements in the "Church-from-below." When both impulses—movements of peoples toward economic, political, and cultural liberation and movements of women toward their own cultural and religious liberation—were joined, a powerful new social force was generated. And within the process, the Mary symbol was shown to have important new potential for the liberation of peoples and for the liberation of women.

Beyond a few statements in *Gaudium et Spes,* the Second Vatican Council failed to deal with the question of women. But it did represent an important transition, by no means yet complete, toward acknowledgement of women in the church in its decision to cast Mary as the central symbol of the human church on its way toward redemption and transformation. For the ambiguities of history and the human struggle of God's lowly ones are aptly joined in the figure of the woman of faith. In ways the council fathers could not foresee, she is being reclaimed by women as a symbol of prophetic possibility for themselves and for the church as a whole. Yes, certain forms of devotion to Mary have diminished—although the rosary has not disappeared as a form of contemplative prayer. Yes, there is a continued ambivalence on the part of Catholics, especially women, toward Marian devotion. There must be, given the passivity, submission, and romantic idealization with which Mary has been endowed. But there is also a restorative side to contemporary interpretations of Mary which show the ancient image as newly provocative in its possibilities for women and for the church today. The Second Vatican Council's depiction of Mary as truly human in her faith, at the heart of the human church, model of the church's final goal and transformation, is open to surprising interpretations today, as Mary is seen in new ways as Seat of Wisdom, Queen of Peace, the Virgin of Guadalupe, Mirror of Justice, Comforter of the Afflicted, symbol of our final freedom in God in her Immaculate Conception and Assumption, as Mother of the Church. Mary is being reclaimed today, especially by women, as a critical symbol in a world where patriarchal models of domination, global warfare, militarism, and hostility are challenged by Christian feminism's personal and political vision of mutuality, reciprocity, cooperation, autonomy in relationship—a love active in the struggles of history. As we interpret the meaning of Mary for our times, in the always new appropriation that is our response to God's living revelation, we participate in the reality to which her symbol points, and we newly discover our relation to her in the mystery of the church.

Footnotes

1　*Chicago Sun Times* (January 25, 1982)

2　Mary Gordon, "Coming to Terms with Mary," *Commonweal* (January 25, 1982), p. 11

3　*Ibid.*

4　*Ibid.*, pp. 11-12; Rosemary Radford Ruether, "Misogynism and Virginal Feminism in the Fathers of the Church," *Religion and Sexism: Images of Women in the Jewish and Christian Traditions* (ed.) Rosemary Radford Ruether (New York: Simon & Schuster, 1974), pp. 150-183, 179

5　Gordon, *ibid.*, p. 12

6　Marina Warner, *Alone of All Her Sex: The Myth and Cult of the Virgin Mary* (New York: Alfred A. Knopf, 1976), pp. 333-339

7　Henry Adams, *The Education of Henry Adams: An Autobiography* (Boston and New York: Houghton Mifflin Co., 1918), pp. 388-389, cited in Mary Daly, *Beyond God the Father: Toward a Philosophy of Women's Liberation* (Boston: Beacon Press, 1973), p. 91

8　Daly, *ibid.*, pp. 91, 82-85

9　Rosemary Radford Ruether, *Mary—The Feminine Face of the Church* (Philadelphia: Westminster, 1977), p. 86

10　Andrew M. Greeley, *The Mary Myth: On the Femininity of God* (New York: Seabury, 1977)

11　Elisabeth Schüssler Fiorenza, "Feminist Spirituality, Christian Identity, and Catholic Vision," *Womanspirit Rising* (eds.) Carol P. Christ and Judith Plaskow (San Francisco: Harper and Row, 1979), pp. 136-148

12　Karl Rahner, "The Theology of Symbol," *Theological Investigations IV* (tr.) Kevin Smyth (Baltimore: Helicon Press, 1966), pp. 221-252; Paul Tillich, *Theology of Culture*, (ed.) Robert C. Kimball (New York: Oxford University Press, 1964), pp. 53-67

13　See Hans Georg Gadamer, *Truth and Method* (New York: Seabury, 1975), section 2 of Part II, pp. 235-344 and Supplement II, pp. 491-498; cf. Paul Ricoeur, *Interpretation Theory: Discourse and the Surplus of Meaning* (Fort Worth: Texas Christian University, 1976), pp. 9-12, 39-95

14　Paul Ricoeur, *Freud and Philosophy: An Essay on Interpretation* (New Haven: Yale University Press, 1970), pp. 3-56, 494-551; *Interpretation Theory: Discourse and the Surplus of Meaning* (Fort Worth: Texas Christian University, 1976), pp. 9-12, 39-95

15　Rt. Rev. Jorge Medina Estevez, "The Blessed Virgin," *Vatican II: An Interfaith Appraisal*, (ed.) John H. Miller (Notre Dame and London: University of Notre Dame Press, 1966), pp. 303-305. Msgr. Estevez was substituting at the Notre Dame conference for Msgr. Gerard Phillips, one of the principal authors of the chapter on Mary in *Lumen Gentium*

16　Albert C. Outler, "A Response," *The Documents of Vatican II* (ed.) Walter M. Abbott, S.J. (tr. ed.) Very Rev. Msgr. Joseph Gallagher (New York: Guild Press, America Press, Association Press, 1966), p. 103

17　Estevez, p. 302

18　Michael Novak, *The Open Church: Vatican II, Act II* (New York: The Macmillan Company, 1964), p. 172

19　*Ibid.*, p. 176

20 *Ibid.*, p. 181
21 *Ibid.*, p. 184
22 *Ibid.*, pp. 184, 201
23 *Ibid.*, p. 182
24 *Ibid.*, pp. 202-203
25 Estevez, *ibid.*, p. 303; others were chapter three of *Lumen Gentium* (on the hierarchy and collegiality), the *Declarations on Religious Liberty and on Non-Christian Religions*, and the first phase of discussion on the *Constitution on Revelation*
26 *Ibid.*, p. 302; cf. also Patrick J. Bearsley, "Mary, the Perfect Disciple," *Theological Studies*, 41:3 (September, 1980), 461-504, 461-463
27 "Dogmatic Constitution on the Church," *The Documents of Vatican II*, #60, pp. 90-91
28 *Ibid.*, #56, p. 88
29 *Ibid.*, #57, #58, #59, pp. 89-90
30 Estevez, p. 306; George Lindbeck, "A Protestant Point of View," *Vatican II: An Interfaith Appraisal*, p. 222
31 "Constitution on the Church," #56, #59
32 *Ibid.*, #58
33 *Ibid.*, #55, #58, #65
34 *Ibid.*, #61
35 *Ibid.*, #62. For an analysis of the recent history, issues, and formation of the texts dealing with the questions of Mary's function, see Michael O'Carroll, "Vatican II and Our Lady's Mediation," *Irish Theological Quarterly*, 37 (1970), pp. 24-55
36 *Ibid.*, #56, #63, #364
37 Estevez, p. 309
38 "Constitution on the Church," #66, #67
39 Estevez, p. 310
40 Henri de Lubac, S.J., "*Lumen Gentium* and the Fathers," *Vatican II: An Interfaith Appraisal*, p. 166
41 "Constitution on the Church," #65
42 *Ibid.*, #68
43 *Ibid.*
44 *Ibid.*
45 *Mary in the New Testament* (eds.) Raymond E. Brown, Karl P. Donfried, Joseph A. Fitzmeyer, John Reumann (Philadelphia: Fortress, 1978), pp. 284, 286
46 *Ibid.*, p. 285
47 *Ibid.*, pp. 285-286
48 *Ibid.*, pp. 287-289
49 Donal Flanagan, *The Theology of Mary* (Hales Corners, WI: Clergy Book Service, 1976), p. 97
50 "Constitution on the Church," #56
51 Flanagan, *ibid.*, pp. 89-97
52 Cf. Patrick J. Bearsley, "Mary, the Perfect Disciple" (note 26, above), presents an excellent analysis of the theme in relation to the NT evidence, but finds it necessary to deny any growth, development, or historical change in Mary's perfection.
53 Cf. e.g. Avery Dulles, S.J., *Models of the Church* (New York: Doubleday, 1974), p. 33 ff; Karl Rahner, "The Church of Sinners" and "The Sinful Church in the Decrees of Vatican II," *Theological Investigations* VI, tr. Karl-H. and Boniface Kruger (Baltimore: Helicon, 1969), pp. 253-269, 270-294

54   Cf. Karl Rahner, "Dogmatic Reflections on the Knowledge and Self-Consciousness of Christ," *Theological Investigations* V, tr. Karl-H. Kruger (Baltimore: Helicon, 1966), pp. 193-215
55   Richard Kugelman, "Presenting Mary to Today's Catholics," *Marian Studies* 22 (Dayton: Mariological Society of America, 1971), p. 53
56   *Ibid.*, pp. 50, 52

MARY, SEAT OF WISDOM, REFLECTION OF THE FEMININITY OF GOD
Margaret I. Healy, BVM

Searching for the origins and meaning of the mystifying title of Mary, Seat of Wisdom, is a challenging task. Neither the theme of wisdom nor the association of Mary with wisdom has been popular in theological, devotional, or historical works in the Roman Church. One medieval artistic representation of Mary, Seat of Wisdom, commands a Golden Portal to the Cathedral of Chartres[1] and holds special significance for our present consideration of Mary's role in the intellectual life of the church. This image of Mary is surrounded by seven feminine figures representing the liberal arts and by seven other figures representing the most learned men of ancient times.

In our own times writings on Mary, particularly the Apostolic Exhortation of Pope Paul VI, *Marialis Cultis,*[2] encourage the study of cultures contemporary to primitive Christianity, along with the art and devotional works of the early Christians. These studies indicate that, even though the Wisdom literature presents convincing evidence, Christianity has consistently rejected the concept of wisdom as the femininity of God, despite some few sound theological writings that supported it, and in so doing have limited Mary's significance for the People of God. In the early '60s, Louis Bouyer wrote a beautiful treatise on wisdom entitled *Mary, Seat of Wisdom,*[3] but the feminine identification of wisdom in the Old Testament was as problematic to him as it seems to have been to most scripture scholars. Henri de Lubac, recently made a cardinal of the church, commented on this in *The Eternal Feminine*:

Perhaps the weakness of most of the current Catholic

theology about Mary is that the authors are unwilling to
take the step that the history of religions enables them to
take and see Mary as a reflection of the femininity of God.
Still, one theologian saw such a step over a half century ago.
Pierre Teilhard de Chardin spoke of the "biopsychological
necessity of the 'Marian' to counterbalance the masculinity
of Yahweh." He argued that the cult of Mary corrects a
"dreadfully masculinized conception of the godhead."[4]

This paper will address briefly four aspects of the topic, Mary, Seat of
Wisdom: Reflection of the Femininity of God:

1. the feminine person in Wisdom literature and some of the guidelines in renewing devotion to Mary;

2. the symbolism of Mary's title, "Seat of Wisdom," and its expression in early Christian art;

3. the difficulties in projecting the Christian message into the Greco-
Roman world and some of the negative consequences;

4. and, finally, the importance for our age of devotion to the Mother
of God under her title, "Seat of Wisdom," important particularly to
Catholic women educators.

The author of the book of Wisdom describes wisdom as "the artificer
of all" (7:22, cf. the "craftsman" in Proverbs 8:30), who teaches all
things to man. This is no difficult task for her since "she penetrates and
pervades all things by reason of her purity" (7:24).

> For she is an aura of the might of God and a pure effusion of
> the glory of the Almighty; therefore nought that is sullied
> enters into her.
> For she is the refulgence of eternal light, the spotless
> mirror of the power of God, the image of his goodness.
> And she, who is one, can do all things, and renews every-
> thing while herself perduring;
> And passing into holy souls from age to age, she produces
> friends of God and prophets.
> For there is nought God loves, be it not one who dwells with
> Wisdom (7:25-28).[5]

The questions of how to identify the feminine in the Wisdom literature and what, if any, relation there is with Mary have been problematic
for scripture scholars. In recent years, however, new approaches to

scriptural and theological studies using recently developed human sciences promise new insights into the Wisdom literature and into the role of Mary in the church. Scholars today, for instance, recognize the significance of ancient religious myths and symbols in both Jewish and Christian traditions. Indeed, the church has come to recognize the significance of all cultural traditions in the religious life of people as it seeks to meet the needs of the people of God.

In one of the most important documents of this century on Mariology, *Marialis Cultis,* Pope Paul VI directed those concerned with renewal of devotion to Mary to follow guidelines from scripture, liturgy, ecumenism, and anthropology.

> What is needed is that texts of prayers and chants should draw their inspiration and their wording from the Bible, and above all that devotion to the Virgin should be imbued with the great themes of the Christian message. This will insure that, as they venerate the Seat of Wisdom, the faithful in their turn will be enlightened by the divine word, and be inspired to live their lives in accordance with the precepts of incarnate wisdom.[6]

In his paper, "Mary in the New Testament and in Catholic Life," Raymond E. Brown, SS, reflecting on his ecumenical efforts in reconciling Catholic and Protestant Marian thought, concluded with this tribute to Pope Paul VI:

> I could not phrase better the result of modern biblical criticism in relation to Mary: "The Virgin Mary has always been proposed to the faithful by the church as an example to be imitated, not precisely in the type of life she led and much less for the socio-cultural background in which she lived and scarcely today exists anywhere. Rather she is held up as an example to the faithful for the way in which in her own particular life she fully and responsibly accepted the will of God, because she heard the word of God and did it. And because charity and the spirit of service were the driving force of her actions. She is worthy of imitation because she was the first and most perfect of Christ's disciples."[7]

Unfortunately, the use of Wisdom references in Marian liturgies has been somewhat confusing. It suggests to some that Mary *is* the feminine person identified as Wisdom in Old Testament Wisdom literature, rather than the *type* of that person. However, today's scripture scholars agree that Wisdom must be identified with divinity. Some scholars maintain that the parallels between the prologue to the gospel of John and Proverbs 8 identify Wisdom with Jesus.[8] Other scholars argue that the Old Testament (Wisdom 9:17) affirms "that this womanly Wisdom represents the [Holy] Spirit."[9] Teilhard de Chardin saw Wisdom as the eternal feminine, "the great hidden force by which everything exists and is made one, bears fruit, moves, is raised up, and is coordinated." In his poem, "The Eternal Feminine," Teilhard's Wisdom, as personified in his Beatrix, tells us, "I am the magnetic force of the universal presence and the ceaseless ripple of its smile. I open the door to the whole heart of creation. . ."[10]

But how is femininity perceived by most humans? Too often in very negative ways. Psychologists tell us that "feminine" characteristics are possessed by both men and women, but in the human experience the "feminine" is chiefly associated with the female of the human species. Consequently, there are those who reduce femininity to femaleness—a serious mistake, particularly when women do it. At the same time, there are humanists who, in their efforts to humanize Mary, almost reduce human femininity to the characteristics of "fallen women." In fact, there are those who react quite negatively to the feminine concept of purity in Mary. Apparently they limit the concept to the physical and/or the sexual. When one reflects on the passage from the Old Testament that is the focus of this paper, it is clear that purity is far more than something physical or sexual. The author of the Book of Wisdom speaks of the purity and femininity of the Divine in these words:

> Wisdom is . . . a pure effusion of the glory of the Almighty; therefore nought that is sullied enters into her . . . she is the *spotless mirror* of the *power of God*, the *image of his goodness*, . . . she, who is *one, can do all things* and *renews everything while herself perduring* (Wisdom 7:25-27).

Mary reflects God's wisdom—the purity, the power, and the goodness of God. Her son, being divine, is Wisdom, but as a human he had to learn from his mother how to express Wisdom as a human. His mother was gifted with Wisdom as God gifts humans, but her gift was, for a human, extraordinary. Mary was chiefly responsible for teaching Jesus. She it was who guided him as he "grew in age, in wisdom, and in grace." She was the teacher of the Great-Teacher-to-Be. When he was a small child, Jesus saw in his mother the Wisdom of God as she reflected to him the power of God, the ability, to his young eyes, to "do all things." He learned goodness from her throughout his life, as she reflected to him the image of God's goodness. And how often did he experience the reflection in her of God's power to "renew everything, while herself perduring."

It is in the Eastern Church that we find the profound and mystical meaning of Mary, Seat of Wisdom. In recalling its ancient traditions, which are also our own, and its great veneration of the glorious Mother of God, the *Theotokos* (the one-bearing-God), we may realize the fulfillment of the hope expressed by Pope Paul VI that we come closer to our brothers and sisters "of the Orthodox churches in which devotion to the Blessed Virgin finds its expression in a beautiful lyricism and in solid doctrine."[11]

Mary's title, "Seat of Wisdom," is rarely used in the Latin or Western Church. In fact, some years ago, the Dominican, Gerald Vann, in criticizing this title in the Litany of Our Lady, commented that "Seat of Wisdom" was hardly a felicitous title. He suggested that it would be better, based on the implications of the Latin *Sedes Sapientiae*, to address her as "Fountain of Wisdom." ". . . The Latin phrase [he commented] would seem to suggest that Mary is the earthly creature in whom above all others wisdom is to be found and from whom above all others it is to be learnt. . ."[12] While I agree with Vann's statement about the implications of the Latin phrase, I disagree with his conclusion to translate it as "Fountain of Wisdom." The symbolism of the word "seat" is quite different from that of the word "fountain" and I suspect that the title originally had both a literal and a symbolic meaning.

The term "seat" has always had significant and honorable meanings. Great universities have been called "seats of learning." Capitols of states and nations are considered "seats of government." While "throne" is associated with kingdom and power, "seat" is usually associated with learning and teaching and usually with non-monarchial governance.

The word "wisdom" in every culture of the Greco-Roman world, pagan or Judeo-Christian, has always suggested a kind of intellectual perfection. In Hebrew history, according to Bouyer, "Wisdom is, essentially, architectonic; it is the art whereby man comes to a knowledge of the world, and to so adapt himself to it . . . that he is enabled to mould history to his own purpose. . . . In Israel, however, . . . Wisdom came to be seen as unattainable by man, except as a gift from God . . . At the final state of a long process of elaboration in the religious thought of Israel, Wisdom becomes, as it were, raised up above the earth and carried up into God."[13]

Wisdom was the gift above all others King Solomon sought from the Lord. "I pleaded and the spirit of Wisdom came to me. I preferred her to scepter and throne, and deemed riches nothing in comparison with her" (Wisdom 7:7-8). Matthew and Luke compare Jesus to Solomon, the sage of the Old Testament: "if the Queen of the South came from the ends of the earth to hear Solomon's wisdom 'behold, a greater than Solomon is here' " (Matthew 12:42; Luke 11:31).

In its liturgy, the church speaks of Wisdom as the gift par excellence of the great Doctors of the Church. In the Common for Doctors, readings are taken from the Book of Wisdom 7:13-14: "What I learned without self-interest, I pass on without reserve; I do not intend to hide Wisdom's riches. For she is an inexhaustible treasure to me, and those who acquire it win God's friendship, commended as they are to him by the benefits of her teaching." And from the Epistle of James (3:17-18) in the same Common of Doctors, we read, "The wisdom that comes down from above is essentially something pure; it also makes for peace, and is kindly and considerate; it is full of compassion and shows itself by doing good. . . . Peacemakers, when they work for peace, sow the seeds which will bear fruit in holiness." Finally, the church relates Wisdom to the role of the Doctor as teacher in her choice of the antiphon: "Those who are learned will be as radiant as the sky in all its beauty; those who instruct the people in goodness will shine like the stars for all eternity."

The Mother of God as "Seat of Wisdom" had a significant place in the early centuries of Christianity, particularly with Christians who governed or who taught or who were recognized as sages or wise men. In one of the very earliest and most common representations of Mary with her child, the Wise Men are offering him gifts from the East. The Christ Child usually is seated on Mary's lap, frequently holding a scroll in his left hand. These representations may be found chiefly on the walls of the catacombs and on the sacarphogi of distinguished people, but there exist today two small ivory carvings of the theme, dated in the early or middle sixth century, that survived the Iconoclasts. One of these is a Justinian ivory, preserved in a museum in Berlin. Its exquisite workmanship identifies it with a workshop in Justinian's Constantinople where the Hellenistic tradition survived in its purest form.[14]

Justinian became emperor of the Eastern Roman Empire in the early part of the sixth century and began immediately to make Constantinople the center of the arts and of learning, initiating a period that is often called the Golden Age of Justinian. One of his major undertakings was to rebuild the great church that Constantine had originally built and dedicated to Holy Wisdom, the Hagia Sophia. A large mosaic in the apse of the vestibule shows Justinian and Constantine proffering gifts to Mary and her son.[15] Constantine's gift is Constantinople, the city he built and from which he ruled the Greco-Roman world. Under his rule the Christians were first freed from persecution and given the rights of citizenship. Justinian offers the Hagia Sophia, so magnificent an edifice that he is said to have exclaimed at its completion, "I have outdone King Solomon." The Virgin and Child in this mosaic are of the type of figure found in early icons. In this mosaic, uncovered in the twentieth century, and in the ancient icons that resemble it, we can discover our mysterious lady, "Seat of Wisdom."

Icons have a very long and important history as religious forms. They are unique to the Eastern Church and partially responsible for the attempted destruction of all religious images by the Iconoclasts in the eighth century. Icons are not ordinary images. In *Theology of the Icon,* Leonid Ouspensky states, the "icon is an image not only of a living but also of a deified prototype. It does not represent the corruptible flesh, destined for decomposition, but transfigured flesh, illuminated by grace, the flesh of the world to come."[16] Icons must be painted in the image and likeness of God. "They are signs of grace and God's presence, of peace, strength, prayerfulness, attention, light."[17]

> The icon is a visible testimony to the descent of God to man
> as well as the impetus of man toward God. . . . If the word
> and the song of the church sanctify our soul by means of
> hearing, the image sanctifies by means of sight, which is,
> according to the Fathers, the most important of the senses.
> . . . The eyes are the light of the body. . . . A true icon
> cannot be created without true knowledge of God. Artistic
> imagination and/or talent cannot replace definite knowl-
> edge. . . ."[18]

Thomas A. Drain has attempted to bridge some of the psychological
gaps existing between the Oriental and Occidental minds as manifested
in their art forms. In an article in *The Marianist,* "Matter and Spirit," he
describes icons of the Virgin and identifies the type of icon that he
believed to be "Mary, Seat of Wisdom."

> . . . The face [Drain tells us] that we see on all the icons of
> the Mother of God is the face developed in the East to show
> most clearly all that she is. She is the "Fiery Chariot of the
> Word of God," the "Hope of Christians," the "Mountain of
> Mercy," the "Warm Intercessor before God," and "Strong
> Protector of the World." Most of all, she is, in the con-
> stantly repeated formula from the divine liturgy of St. John
> Chrysostom, "the all-holy, the most highly blessed, our
> glorious Lady, the Mother of God and ever-Virgin, Mary."
> What all these various Eastern titles seek to tell us about
> our Lady, the icon-painter must show in her face.[19]

Drain goes on to describe Mary's traditional clothing, typical of
women's clothing in the Constantinian Empire. Mary usually wears an
ankle-length blue-gray tunic with tight sleeves. A light blue cloth cap
completely covers her hair. The *maphorion,* a large deep red veil bor-
dered in gold, enfolds the entire person. Three gold stars, symbolic of
Mary's virginity before, during, and after the birth of Jesus, decorate the
head and shoulders of the *maphorion.* Mary always wears a large golden
halo. Gold and colored embroidery usually decorate her shoes. Four
Greek letters, the first and last letters of the two words "Mother of
God," complete the icon.

In the icons identified as "Seat of Wisdom," Jesus is seated on the lap
of his mother or on her arm. He is dressed in the robes of a teacher and

carries in his left hand a closed scroll, the symbol of a distinguished teacher who has the power to open the scroll and reveal the meaning within. His right hand is raised in blessing with two fingers touching, symbolic of the two natures in Christ, and the other three fingers extended, symbolic of the three unique Divine Persons in the Trinity. On the nimbus that surrounds his head is imprinted the cross. His figure is larger than that of a child. His features are mature and resemble those of his mother. Both mother and child look outward toward the worshipper. It is significant that neither mother nor child wears a crown. The artist shows Jesus as the Divine Teacher, not a king. Mary is mother and teacher, not a queen-mother. (Some of the beautiful ancient icons that survived the Iconoclasts have been spoiled by superimposing crowns on the heads of Jesus and Mary.)

The icon "Seat of Wisdom" is particularly rich in mystical meaning and calls forth profound reflection on the mysteries surrounding the *theotokos* (the-one-bearing-God), mother and teacher of Jesus, the Great Teacher. It reminds us that "she pondered all these things in her heart" (Luke 2:51) and the mystery of "these things" is expressed by the artist in her eyes. Mary points to her son, the Divine Teacher. He is represented in a position of dependence on her, dependent for many human things, but particularly dependent upon his mother for manifesting and helping him to manifest God's Wisdom, the femininity of Divinity itself. Mary's figure is larger than life, a figure of power and strength, of peace and of great compassion.

Icons were only one form of the art in the ancient church that, next to the spoken word, was the chief means of educating the people. The song and chant of liturgical prayer and worship, images and representations of Christ's life on walls, painted and/or woven, sculpture, carvings, and mosaics—all were used to teach the Christian message that Jesus Christ was the long-awaited Messiah, the Son of God, true God and true Man, was born of a woman in Bethlehem, manifested himself to the Wise Men of the East (the non-Hebrew world), lived and taught in Galilee, died on a cross, and rose from the dead to save all people. But it is important for us to realize that this message was projected into a world dominated by Roman law, Greek language and learning, and pagan religions. It is probable that pagan religions were of special significance in the rejection of Wisdom as the femininity of God.

Mystery cults and the cults of the great mother goddesses, particularly that of the Egyptian Isis, prevailed among many intellectuals throughout the Greco-Roman world, influencing in some ways even the Jews who, by the time of Christ, had been scattered in colonies throughout the Hellenized world. At the same time, many intellectuals, through the Greek philosophers, had come to believe in one supreme transcendent Being, even as the Jews, through their prophets, had come to believe in the one God, Yahweh. Nonetheless, the ancient worship of many deities was still an almost universal reality. Humankind from primitive times had to find an explanation for transcendent powers and phenomena they could not understand. Only in feminine deities could some of these be explained.

In his book, *Primitive Christianity in Its Contemporary Setting,* published in 1965, Rudolf Bultmann described the changing religious convictions of intellectuals and other leaders of the Greco-Roman world:

> Clearly, among the mystery religions, especially those which hailed from Egypt, there grew up a form of worship and devotion hitherto unparalleled in Greco-Roman antiquity . . . it would be true to say that the spread of the mystery religions is symptomatic of the change in the general view of life which had come over the Greco-Roman world.[20]

According to Bultmann, people had become very uncertain about their relation to their world. Neither the performance of civic duty nor intellectual contemplation of the world and its unity nor appreciation of the universal Logos as rational law of nature could satisfy the inner longing for harmony and peace. Some deity above the world, coming in mystery, was considered more and more as the only answer to the human predicament and quest.

The most pervasive of the mystery religions in the Greco-Roman world was that of the cult of the Egyptian goddess Isis. Her importance to all segments of society is revealed in the works of the Egyptian poet and melodist, Isidorus. (Some of his hymns are preserved in the original papyrus copies.) In one of these hymns to Isis, Isidorus reveals the powerful position of the Egyptian goddess of Wisdom in the lives of the people of his time.

O wealth-giver, Queen of the gods, Hermouthis, Lady,
Omnipotent Agathe Tyche, greatly renowned Isis,
Deo, highest Discoverer of all life,
manifold miracles were Your care that You might bring
5 livelihood to mankind and morality to all;
  [and] You taught customs that justice might in some
    measure prevail;
You gave skills that men's life might be comfortable,
and You discovered the blossoms that produce edible
    vegetation.
Because of You heaven and the whole earth have their
    being;
10 And the gusts of the winds and the sun with its sweet
    light.
By Your power the channels of Nile are filled, every
    one,
At the harvest season and its most turbulent water is
    poured
On the whole land that produce may be unfailing.
All mortals who live in the boundless earth,
15 Thracians, Greeks and Barbarians,
Express Your Fair Name, a Name greatly honoured
    among all, [but]
Each [speaks] in his own language, in his own land.
The Syrians call You: Astarte, Artemis, Nanaia,
The Lycian tribes call You: Leto, the Lady,
20 The Thracians also name You as Mother of the gods,
And the Greeks [call You] Hera of the Great Throne,
    Aphrodite,
Hestia the goodly, Rheia and Demeter.
But the Egyptians call You "Thiouis" [because they
    know] that You, being One, are all
Other goddess' invoked by the races of men.
25 Mighty One, I shall not cease to sing of Your great
    Power,
Deathless Saviour, many-named, mightiest Isis,
Saving from war, cities and all their citizens:

Men, their wives, possessions, and children.
As many as are bound fast in prison, in the power of
death,
30 As many as are in pain through long, anguished, sleep-
less nights,
All who are wanderers in a foreign land,
And as many as sail on the Great Sea in winter
When men may be destroyed and their ships wrecked
and sunk . . .
All [these] are saved if they pray that You be present to
help.
35 Hear my prayers, O One Whose Name has great Power;
Prove Yourself merciful to me and free me from all
distress.

Isidorus[21]

Recognizing this widespread devotion to the Great Goddess, Isis, we should not be surprised that a feminine deity is found in the Hebrew Wisdom literature. Does not Isidorus reveal what must have been a climate of religious belief that was perceived by St. Paul and many of the earliest Christian leaders to be a threat to the acceptance of Jesus Christ as Savior, Messiah, and Son of God? Can it explain why St. Paul's only reference to the mother of Jesus was to emphasize the human nature of her son?[22]

Christians and Jews today are familiar with Yahwehism and the stumbling block it has been to the acceptance of Jesus Christ by the Jews as the Messiah. Most of the world is familiar with the philosophy of the Greeks. Its influence has surely affected the thinking of the Roman Church, particularly through St. Augustine and St. Thomas Aquinas. Roman power and law have contributed to the bureaucratic and legalistic functioning of the Roman Church. But there has been little recognition of the negative impact on Christianity of the ancient and almost universal worship of a powerful feminine deity. The early Christians' rejection of a feminine deity has resulted, in the words of Teilhard, in a "dreadfully masculinized conception of the Godhead."[23]

Bultmann's description of intellectuals in the Greco-Roman world could just as well describe many intellectuals today. Disillusionment with the human ability to solve the problems of the world, entrapment of masses of people in different kinds of paganisms, continuing struggles and wars for power and wealth—all these were experiences and concerns of thoughtful men and women prior to and during the early years of Christianity. Today we share all these concerns, but probably for many the threat of the awful consequences of a nuclear holocaust overshadows them all. We are no doubt in the midst of the greatest power struggle in the history of the human race. In our concern over the nuclear build-up and the growing power-threat to the very existence of the world, are we overlooking the source of that great power? It is not in the stockpiles of nuclear weapons or in the marvels of modern technology. It is in the human intellect, the supreme human instrument of power, which attains its perfection through wisdom—created wisdom, yes, but most important through Uncreated Wisdom.

Through the ages, the intellect has been used and abused in the human quest for knowledge, happiness, and power of every kind. It was the faculty that masterminded in this century the Communist revolution and the subjugation of nations to Communist power. It was the power that carried out the Holocaust in Europe. It is the power that has developed and used our nuclear weapons. Indeed, it is the power that has given rise to most of the problems of our world today. These problems will be solved only if our intellectual resources are developed and informed by the Wisdom of God, for the intellect is also the power for creating peace and justice and all good things.

Time does not permit a review of the history of the development of the intellect of humankind. Anthropologists, psychologists, sociologists, historians, and others are doing this. But it would be helpful if our memories could make only a cursory review of the efforts that kings, emperors, and nations have made through the centuries to develop the intellects of their people in order to improve the quality of their lives and of their countries or, on the other hand, to curb this development and subjugate a people. To foster Christianity we know that great universities, schools, and centers of learning have been developed, encouraged, and supported. We also know that even in our own time rulers of countries have confiscated these institutions and have banned the teaching of Christianity. There is a great need today to reflect very seriously on these realities and to examine the critical need for educators—Catholic educators with new vision inspired by the Wisdom of God.

Many scholars of different disciplines are addressing the pheno-menon of social and technological change in our times. The insights of some modern physicists are particularly significant. One such is Fritjof Capra, author of *The Turning Point: Science, Society and the Rising Culture*. The message of his book is condensed in his article in the De-cember 1982 *Futurist*, "The Turning Point: A New Vision of Reality." In it he makes some very important observations.

> We live in a globally interconnected world, in which biolog-ical, psychological, social, and environmental phenomena are all interdependent. . . . A massive shift in the percep-tion of reality is underway, with thinkers in many disci-plines beginning to move away from the traditional reduc-tionist, mechanical world view to an ecological, holistic systems paradigm.[24]

The crises of our times are essentially part of the same crisis, "essen-tially [Capra believes] a crisis of perception."

> We are trying to apply the concepts of an outdated world view—the mechanistic world view of Cartesian-Newtonian science—to a reality that can no longer be understood in these terms. . . . over-emphasis on the Cartesian method has led to the fragmentation characteristic of both our gen-eral thinking and our academic disciplines and to the wide-spread attitude of reductionism in science.[25]

Some of the most serious consequences of this fragmentation and reductionism, according to Capra, have been experienced by many of us in modern medical practices; they have been observed, as well as exper-ienced, by most of us in the failure of economic theory to solve the problems of a fundamentally interdependent world.

Capra decried the fact that most economists still consider undifferen-tiated economic, technological, and institutional growth as a sign of healthy economy, even though such growth is causing "ecological disas-ters, widespread corporate crime, social disintegration, and the ever-increasing likelihood of nuclear war." Unfortunately, economists are accepting without question the "highly imbalanced set of values that dominates our culture."[26]

Capra used the *yin-yang* concept of the Chinese to describe this "imbalanced value system." *Yin* values have been neglected and rejected in favor of *yang* values and attitudes. Complementarity and harmonious balance have been lost in the preference for "self-assertion over integration, analysis over synthesis, rational knowledge over intuitive wisdom, science over religions, competition over cooperation, expansion over conservation." Such imbalance has led us to the brink of nuclear destruction. This *yang*-oriented value system supported by patriarchy must now give way to the feminist perspective characterizing *yin* values. A harmonious balance must be restored.[27]

Finally, Capra noted the beginning of a significant shift in values, indicated by new appreciations of voluntary simplicity rather than material consumption, of inner growth and development rather than economic and technological growth, of "small is beautiful" rather than large-scale enterprises and institutions. Feminist awareness, originating in the women's movement, may well become the catalyst for many other movements coalescing to "re-emphasize the quest for meaning and the spiritual dimension of life."[28]

In this social transformation that is taking place, how significant will be the role of women called to influence the development of the intellectual life of present and future generations.[29] How significant will be the role of those committed to the best of the women's movement—that is, exploring, discovering, and communicating the feminine dimension of God. How important should be Mary's role as Seat of Wisdom!

A new Marian age must dawn in the church and a new thrust in education must be made as we begin to reflect more on the demands this society-in-transformation has placed on educators and on the need for the inspiration of that strong and compassionate Woman who has hidden within her the feminine mystery of God. We need Mary to remind us that God's Wisdom is essential to solving the problems of our world. We need her to help us to discover the meaning and significance of the femininity of God, to discover that God's Wisdom is expressed particularly in Mary's Divine Son as the Great and Good Teacher; but we need to remember that Jesus continues to depend upon his mother, his "first and greatest disciple," and upon his other women disciples, to exemplify the femininity of the Divine. We need Mary to

remind us of the words from the Book of Wisdom telling us that the
Femininity of Divinity, or Divine Wisdom

> . . . is the artificer of all (Wisdom 7:22) . . . who teaches
> all things to man. . . .
> She (it is who) penetrates and pervades all things by reason
> of her purity (Wisdom 7:24). . . .
> For she is the aura of the might of God
>   and a pure effusion of the glory of the Almighty;
>   therefore nought that is sullied enters into her.
> For she is the refulgence of eternal light,
>   the spotless mirror of the power of God,
>   the image of his goodness.
> And she, who is one, can do all things,
>   and renews everything while herself perduring;
> And passing into holy souls from age to age,
>   she produces friends of God and prophets.
> For there is nought God loves
>   be it not one who dwells with Wisdom.
>
> (Wisdom 7:25-28)

Footnotes

1   Rene Merlet, *The Cathedral of Chartres* (Paris: Henri Laurens, Publisher), 1926, pp.
    30-32
2   Pope Paul VI, *Marialis Cultis* (Washington, D.C.: United States Catholic Conference
    Publications Office), 1974, #29
3   Louis Bouyer, *Mary, Seat of Wisdom,* (trans.) Fr. A.V. Littledale (New York: Pan-
    theon Books), 1962, pp. 194, 196
    Bouyer's chapter on "Wisdom and the Assumption" is particularly relevant to this
    paper and it reflects the problem of masculinizing the feminine Wisdom. He stated,
    "Wisdom is in God, is of God, and nothing can be that without being God *himself.*
    Yet Wisdom is that in God whereby he is concerned in his creation, comprehends it
    in the fullest sense of the word, loves it with the very love by which he lives in loving
    himself. Wisdom, then, in its first aspect, appears impossible to distinguish really
    from the divine essence; but, in another aspect, it is that in God which leads to the
    distinction of creature and Creator, but to this distinction as surmounted, if not abol-
    ished, by the divine love. Wisdom is identical with the divine essence, but as partici-

pable by creatures, as comprising the possibility, realized by the divine mind and will, of their distinct existence. At the same time, it comprises this existence of theirs as merged again in the divine life, taken hold of again, in its distinctness, by the divine love" (p. 19). ". . . Wisdom is not confined to a single personal realisation in history. It will comprise, while preserving their distinctness, all those who are saved in the actual course of history, all who have attained to the filial status shared by so many *brethren* in the Only Beloved. . . . More particularly, the Spouse, along with their husband himself, is to be, as it were, made ready and brought into being by the mother from whom all motherhood on earth proceeds, within time, in view of eternity. Her final realisation as Virgin and Spouse, at the end of time, is therefore not only prefigured but precontained in an antecedent realisation, in the middle of time, as Virgin Mother. It is strictly in this aspect that Mary is not the final or complete realisation of Wisdom, but its supreme realisation on the plane of history. Mary is truly the Seat of Wisdom, of the uncreated Wisdom shown forth as a creature in her Son who is, at the same time, Son of the *Father*; and she is, thereby, the source, within history, of the eschatological Wisdom, created in time to espouse in time its eternal realisation in the Son who is the Word" (p. 196, italics added).

4 Henri de Lubac, *The Eternal Feminine*, (trans.) Rene Hauge (New York: Harper and Row Publishers), 1971, pp. 125-6
5 R.E. Murphy, *Seven Books of Wisdom* (Milwaukee: The Bruce Publishing Co.), 1960, p. 146
6 Pope Paul VI, *ibid.*, #30
7 Raymond E. Brown, "Mary in the New Testament and in Catholic Life," *America*, May 15, 1982, p. 379
8 R.E. Murphy, "Wisdom (in the Bible)," *New Catholic Encyclopedia*, #14, 1967, p. 146
9 Yves Congar, "The Spirit as God's Feminity," *Theology Digest* (30:2), Summer, 1982, pp. 129-132
   Both Congar's short article, "The Spirit as God's Femininity," and Dietschy's article, "God Is Father and Mother," in the issue of *Theology Digest* cited, are very short but well worth reading.
10 Lubac, *ibid.*, p. 25
11 Pope Paul VI, *ibid.*, #32
12 Gerald Vann, "Notes of Our Lady's Litany," *Worship*. Vol. xxx, 1955, p. 440
13 Bouyer, *ibid.*, p. 191
14 Kurt Weitzmann (ed.), *Age of Spirituality—Late Antique and Early Christian Art. Third to Seventh Century*. Catalog of the exhibition at the Metropolitan Museum of Art. November 19, 1977, through February 12, 1978 (New York: Princeton University Press, 1979), p. 529
15 Lord Kinross and Newsweek Book Division (eds.), *Hagia Sophia* (New York: Newsweek, 1972), p. 128
16 Leonid Ouspensky, *Theology of the Icon* (Crestwood, New York: St. Vladimir's Seminary Press, 1978), p. 191
17 *Ibid.*, p. 192
18 *Ibid.*, p. 227
19 Thomas A. Drain, "Matter and Spirit," *Marianist*, 1963, p. 25 (passim). The Marianist 54, January-February, 1963
20 Rudolf Bultmann, *Primitive Christianity in Its Contemporary Setting* (New York: The World Publishing Co., 1965), pp. 160-161

21   Vera F. Vanderlip, *American Studies in Papyrology*, Vol. 12, *The Four Greek Hymns of Isidorus and the Cult of Isis* (Toronto: A.M. Hakkert, Ltd., 1972), pp. 18-19

22   Rene Laurentin, "Jesus and Women: An Underestimated Revolution," *Concilium: Women in a Men's Church*, v. 134. According to Laurentin, "So much had to be done to compel recognition of the glory of Jesus in face of objections from so many mortal enemies that they had to choose the points on which to fight, to gain acceptance of the essential without provoking, on the subject of women, the kind of irresistible outcry which was so familiar to the preachers of the gospel, such as the apostle Paul at Athens (Acts 17:32-34)." (Seabury Press: New York, N.Y., 1980), p. 82

23   Lubac, *ibid.*, p. 126

24   Fritjof Capra, "The Turning Point: A New Vision of Reality," *The Futurist*, Vol. xvi, No. 6, p. 19 (December, 1982)

25   *Ibid.*, p. 19

26   *Ibid.*, pp. 20-21

27   *Ibid.*, p. 21. "From the earliest times of Chinese culture, *yin* has . . . been associated with the feminine and *yang* with the masculine."

28   *Ibid.*, p. 24

29   John Naisbit, *Megatrends* (New York: Warner Books, Inc., 1982).

       In this book the author discusses what he called "Ten New Directions Transforming Our Lives." He concluded, "We are living in the *time of the parenthesis*, the time between eras. It is as though we have bracketed off the present from both the past and the future, for we are neither here nor there. . . .

       "As we move from an industrial to an information society, we will use our brain-power to create instead of our physical power, and the technology of the day will extend and enhance our mental ability" (p. 249). And, in another place, he said, "We are moving in the dual direction of high tech/high touch, matching each new technology with a compensatory human response" (p. 1).

       "Although the time between eras is uncertain, it is a great and yeasty time, filled with opportunity. If we can learn to make uncertainty our friend, we can achieve much more than in stable eras.

       "In stable eras, everything has a name and everything knows its place, and we can leverage very little.

       "But in the time of the parenthesis [the time between eras] we have extraordinary leverage and influence—individually, professionally, and institutionally—if we can only get a clear sense, a clear conception, a clear vision, of the road ahead.

       "My God, what a fantastic time to be alive!" (p. 252).

COMFORTER OF THE AFFLICTED: CHRISTIAN PASTORAL CARE AND NEW MINISTRIES FOR WOMEN

Rose Marie Lorentzen, BVM

"Comforting the afflicted" captures the dynamic of God's salvific relationship with humanity. In the Hebrew scriptures, prophets carried out God's mission of comforting the afflicted. We who are disciples of Jesus Christ are also asked to enter into this prophetic mission. Mary, who is the prototype[1] of discipleship, symbolizes what we are all called to be. This basic summary of the theme of this paper presupposes several scriptural premises.

The earliest gospel account, that of Mark, presents an unfavorable portrait of both Mary and the brothers. Matthew's portrayal of Mary is somewhat more favorable, and in Luke, Mary moves into the role of paradigm; she is the model disciple *par excellence*, the one who does the word. In John, the Mother of Jesus and the Beloved Disciple, the two characters never named, both take on the role of paradigm.

According to some scholars, neither in the three Synoptics nor in John can one find a verifiable basis for assuming that Mary became a disciple prior to the Resurrection; the evidence, in fact, points in quite the opposite direction. What can be known about the development of Mary in Christian scriptures is that Mary probably was not a disciple during the lifetime of Jesus,[2] but she did belong to the Christian community after the Resurrection. At that point, John presents her as the epitome of Christian discipleship.[3]

The New Testament writers did not give the title "Comforter of the Afflicted" to Mary. Mary is more clearly portrayed as "the afflicted" (in Luke) and as the disciple of Lady Wisdom who is strengthened and enlivened by the Comforter, the Spirit/Paraclete (in John).[4]

A virtual lacuna exists connecting the Mary of scipture with any title similar to "Comforter of the Afflicted." Absence of Marian texts other than the gospels and Apocalypse frustrates attempts to discover any Marian memories in the earliest Christian community. Second-century references to Mary were largely polemical or allegorical; patristic writers mentioned Mary only to clarify their Christological concerns.

However, three reasons emerged that prompted me to pursue some scriptural and theological understanding for this Marian title: Mary's gradual historical emergence as the feminine face of God; the rich nuance underlying this title, Comforter of the Afflicted; and growing scholarly awareness of Mary's role as disciple with all the prophetic aspects that title includes.

Very early in church history, writers began drawing parallels between Christ and Mary. Jesus mirrors God's attributes and carries on God's mission; Mary mirrors Jesus as he mirrors God. Moreover, as Jesus becomes more and more removed from the human realm, as he becomes increasingly austere and beyond people's reach, Mary is endowed with the divine characteristics of love and faithfulness (*hesed, emet*).[5]

It seems reasonable to assume that "Comforter of the Afflicted" belongs to that vast store of symbolism surrounding the godhead that eventually becomes transferred to Mary in an attempt to recapture the feminine aspects of the divine. Mary mirrored God for ordinary people. Popular devotion to her preserved in our folk memory the image of a compassionately loving and involved God. Mary became the feminine face of God.

Though the history of title, "Comforter of the Afflicted," is obscure during the Christian era, the roots of the phrase in the prophetic and Wisdom traditions of the Hebrew scriptures are quite clear. Clues to links between the Hebrew and Christian scriptures' use and understanding of Comforter of the Afflicted are myriad. A rich complex of prophetic and Wisdom traditions undergird both Luke's and John's theologies. As we shall see, in Second Isaiah "Comforter of the Afflicted" describes God's way of dealing with humanity. In this Isaian theology it is God who comforts her children and, in the Servant Songs, she calls on her prophet-servant to do likewise.[6] For Isaiah, comfort is equivalent to salvation! The term is reinterpreted in the Wisdom tradition where Lady Wisdom also assumes the prophetic task of comforting.

In other words, "Comforter of the Afflicted" captures the dynamic of God's relationship to humanity and, therefore, describes the role of a prophet, one who takes on God's most essential concern, to change unloving and unjust structures to make God's peaceable new world a reality. The Johannine author was strongly influenced by Wisdom literature and the vision of Second Isaiah.[7] In the fourth gospel, this vision permeates both the understanding of discipleship and of the Spirit/Paraclete.

Both Luke and John present Mary in the context of discipleship. A disciple walks "on the way" of Jesus (Luke) and does "even greater things" than he (John). Mary in relation to discipleship, then, can give us further scriptural insight into our own present-day share in the prophetic mission of Christ.

After denying any overt attempt by the evangelists to call Mary "Comforter of the Afflicted," I would nevertheless suggest that, as prototype of disciple, called to carry on Christ's mission, Mary does take on the prophetic task. She (and we) take on God's mission of "Comforting the Afflicted." It is my goal here to show how that happens.

The Influence of Second Isaiah

The "Comforter" God we meet in Isaiah is the feminine face of God. How does God comfort? God comforts as a mother. God comforts with unending compassion. God comforts by confronting injustice and unfreedom. Giving comfort, in fact, is "God's proper work."[8] In an image so central to this prophetic proclamation, Second Isaiah deliberately describes God in language that unites feminine and prophetic imagery. Because Second Isaiah was a major influence in the Lukan and Johannine communities, its image of "prophetic comfort" does not deserve to be relegated to the periphery of Christian consciousness.[9] Consider Isaiah's vision for a moment, a vision in which "comfort" is a prophetic word calling us to confront radically a distinctly un-comfortable world.

The dominant motif of Second Isaiah is introduced in its hope-filled opening words: "Comfort, comfort my people, says your God" (Isaiah 40:1).[10] Because Second Isaiah is one major source of inspiration for the Johannine Paraclete,[11] this text can enrich our understanding of Paraclete as used here and in John. God calls the prophet to be comforter. That link is vital for understanding the call of Mary and other disciples in the fourth gospel.

Using covenant language, the prophet sings the joyous news of God's coming in glory (40:12-31). God is Israel's everlasting creator and sustainer to whom none can compare. Israel will see a new act from God: a new creation and a new exodus. Their God will empower them and sustain them always.

As Isaiah continues, we discover God appearing in courts of law—the god of gods engaging in disputes with gods of other nations (41:1ff), listening to the complaints of Israel, and finally promising: "Therefore hear this, you who are afflicted. . . . Thus says your Lord, the Lord your God who pleased the cause of his people" (51:21a). Why can Israel take comfort? Because God has come forth as its advocate.

In a later text, Yahweh further promises that Israel can indeed take comfort: "For the Lord has *comforted* his people, God has *redeemed* Jerusalem. . . . And all the ends of the earth shall see the *salvation* of our God" (52:9-10). The author used the Hebraic technique of poetic parallelism here to show that "comfort" is equivalent to being redeemed—to "salvation." Once again, the Isaian theme reappears. How does a god give comfort? By promising the inbreaking of *Shalom*— God's new era of peace and justice, truth and love extending to "all the ends of the earth."

Other Isaian texts portray God as a mother who comforts her children. After reiterating the promise that Yahweh will lead a New Exodus to manifest her endless compassion (49:7-12), a triumphant Hymn of Comfort proclaims:

> Sing for joy, O heavens, and exult, O earth;
> break forth, O mountains, into singing!
> For Yahweh (a) has comforted (b)*the people*
> (b¹) and *upon the afflicted* (a¹) will show compassion
> (49:13b).

Trible points out that the Hebrew word here translated "compassion" is a maternal metaphor with rich connotations. The singular noun (*rehem*) means "womb"; the plural means "compassion, mercy, and love." The adjective (which is used only to refer to God) is "merciful or gracious"; and the verb, "to show mercy."

Study of the parallels in this text shows that to be comforted by Yahweh (a) is to know God's compassion—to experience love emanating from the very womb of God (a¹). Those encompassed by God's compassion are the people (b) who are afflicted (b¹). When the people hesitate in accepting this promise, Yahweh gives even profounder commitment: "Can a woman forget her sucking child, that she should have no compassion on the son of her womb?" (49:15a).

Yet even this fullness of maternal love, to which God lays claim, cannot exhaust the depths of compassion with which God increasingly reaches out to the afflicted: "Even these may forget, yet I will not forget you!" (49:15b). Indeed, God's compassion extends throughout life. "Even to your old age I am the same, even when your hair is gray I will bear you; It is I who have done this, I who will continue, and I who will carry you to safety" (46:3-4). Reflecting on the rich imagery of this maternal metaphor, Trible concluded:

> To the responsive imagination, this metaphor suggests the
> meaning of love as selfless participation in life. The womb
> protects and nourishes but does not possess and control. It
> yields its treasure in order that wholeness and well-being
> may happen. Truly, it is the way of compassion.[12]

Second Isaiah also makes another significant Hebrew term, *hesed*, equivalent to "compassion." Since "compassion" is synonymous with "comfort," understanding the term *hesed*, God's compassion for the afflicted, will further our understanding of both terms:

"With ⟮EVERLASTING LOVE (*hesed*)
I will have ⟍COMPASSION on you" (54:8b).

Hesed is sometimes translated as "mercy," other times as "pity," more often as "steadfast and enduring love." It also meant *grace* to the believing Israelite. But all of our English translations lack the dimension of action that the Hebrew word implies. Jose Miranda; the liberation theologian, translates *hesed* as "interhuman compassion." This biblical compassion is an unreserved commitment to the weak, the poor, and the oppressed. It is identical to an absolute sense of justice; it is, in fact, "love-justice" and calls for action on behalf of the poor and the oppressed. Above all, *hesed* affirms the centrality of God's gracious love—a graciousness that cares and asks and expects much from us.[13]

Second Isaiah makes clear that God comforts the people by promising the arrival of the day of *Shalom*. God comes forth as Israel's advocate to call for peace and justice in the land. Not only does God extend endless loving justice and compassion, God also calls on the prophet-servant to do the same and promises the fullness of God's spirit to engage in this crucial mission. The servant "will not fail or be discouraged [i.e., lack in comfort] till he has established justice on the earth" (42:4). The servant will accomplish this in a most gentle, nonviolent manner, breaking not the bruised reed. Rather, this prophet will rouse the weary with words of compassion and comfort (50:4-9).

Isaiah does not limit this vital prophetic role to one servant, however. All in Israel are challenged to be prophet-servants, not only for the nation, but also in terms of responsibility for the world that "salvation [i.e., comfort] may reach to the end of the earth" (49:6).

How then does God comfort? God comforts by sending forth prophet-servants to bring loving-justice to the land. The fullness of God's blessing, of God's promise, flows freely from God's prophets to all the people of the earth.

Comfort in the Wisdom and Johannine Traditions

The vision of "prophetic comfort" put forth in Isaiah is related to the Wisdom tradition, particularly in a text Riesenfeld believed to be the key to the Johannine Paraclete. In Proverbs 8, the words of comfort that Yahweh, and then the prophet-servant, had addressed to Israel are now reinterpreted in the discourse of Lady Wisdom who extends comfort to all of humanity: "It is you, O men, whom I comfort, and I direct my voice to the sons of men" (Proverbs 8:4ff). Lady Wisdom now takes on the role of Yahweh. The way in which she extends comfort is not quite what we might expect, however. In Wisdom, comfort is synonymous with teaching, showing what is right and denouncing what is wrong. In other words, the Wisdom tradition continues to use "comfort" to describe a prophetic mission.

Riesenfeld asserted that striking similarities exist between personified Wisdom in Proverbs—with all its resonance of the Isaian comforter—and the Paraclete/comforter in John. He considered it quite probable that those texts that describe the comforting functions of Wisdom are the source of the Johannine Paraclete who is the Spirit of Truth.[14] If Riesenfeld is correct, and scholars seem increasingly convinced of the significant influence of both the prophetic and wisdom traditions in all four gospels,[15] then the entire Wisdom tradition, as well as Second Isaiah, should be kept in mind as we begin to examine the role of the Johannine Paraclete.

John's gospel draws significant parallels between the sending of the Spirit and the sending of the disciples. The functions assigned to the Paraclete are precisely the functions assigned by the gospel to the disciples.[16] We have no exact synonym for the term *Parakletos* as used by John. The word really has no Hebrew equivalent, although both John and Luke are clearly influenced by the Isaian portrayal of God as a mother who comforts her children. The Greek term common to John's milieu had a variety of distinct meanings, all of which John probably intended to evoke. Helpful insight can be gained by examining briefly key passages in the Farewell Discourses of the fourth gospel, which contain five Paraclete sayings (14:15-17; 14:25-26; 15:26-27; 16:7-11; 16:12-14). The Johannine Paraclete is described as Advocate/Counselor, Intecessor/Mediator, Comforter/Consoler, and Exhorter/Stimulator/Encourager/Life-Giver.[17]

Advocate/Counselor

In ancient Israel a judge, sometimes the king, used to act as an attorney endeavoring to bring justice to the oppressed. In Isaiah, we saw Yahweh as Advocate for Israel; in John, the Paraclete takes on that role in two ways. First, the Paraclete pleads Jesus' case, defending him and acting as a witness at his trial (John 14:16). The defense's task is to testify that Jesus is the true victor. The Paraclete also serves as a prose-

cuting attorney who puts the world on trial, convicting it of sin (16:7-
11).

During Jesus' life, his very presence had highlighted the contrast
between his words and deeds and the dismal reality of a sinful world.
When he leaves, the Paraclete will continue the critical ministry of
convicting the world of its sin, its self-righteousness, and its unbelief or,
as John puts it, "sin, righteousness, and judgment"—three basic motifs
of prophetic proclamation.[18]

Intercessor/Mediator

This Paraclete saying deals with Jesus' approaching death and the
passing on of his teaching mission through the Paraclete:
> These things I have spoken to you, while abiding with you.
> But the paraclete, the holy spirit, whom the father will send
> in my name, will teach you all things, and bring to your
> remembrance all that I have said to you (14:25-26).

Because the Paraclete will pass on to them the message of Jesus and
explain to them what Jesus meant, his disciples will be able to perceive
more than was possible for Jesus' contemporaries. Indeed, the Paraclete
will empower disciples faithfully to carry on their own ministry as true
witness/prophets (15:26-27).

The Paraclete will also disclose to them what is to come, another
prophetic aspect of the Paraclete's role. Jesus' spirit engages in no rote
passing on of Jesus' message, however. Rather, the nature of prophecy
compels the Paraclete to alter, amend, and even authorize "new words
of Jesus for new and unprecedented times."[19] This is strong scriptural
reassurance, backing the quest of today's feminist theologians for "new
words of Jesus" for our times.

Comforter/Consoler

During the Farewell Discourse, Jesus told his disciples that he was
leaving them, that they must witness to him, and that they also would
be persecuted. Small wonder they were discouraged. But Jesus reassures

them; he will send a comforter to strengthen them. The Paraclete will take his place in their lives, will live in them, and will help them carry out their mission of witnessing to and confronting an imperfect world. As should be quite clear by now, this promise of comfort never implies an end to the suffering inherent in the prophetic task. Rather, the comfort is that the disciples are not left alone; the Spirit-Paraclete will be working within and through them, enabling them to know all truth and empowering them to do far *greater works than even Jesus* did (John 14:12). This promise of the disciple being able to outshine the leader is particularly characteristic of the Johannine gospel. We are usually well aware that John has a high Christology, but often lose sight of the fact that he has an equally high anthropology. Whatever marvelous things John proclaims about the Lord, he proclaims possible for Mary and other disciples as well.

Exhorter/Stimulator/Encourager/Life-Giver

John concludes his gospel with a dynamic outward impulse: the young Christian community is not to look backward but to move into the future. In a certain sense, the community is living in God's future even now. Jesus himself was sent to reveal God—the Comforter-God who cares for the poor and sends forth prophets to carry on God's mission. In John's gospel, Jesus too sends forth disciples. Now disciples are sent to continue God's mission of bestowing comfort/salvation to all in the name of Jesus Christ.

The community's stance toward the world, then, is one of outreach and responsibility. The Spirit-Paraclete is present as stimulator and encourager, acting as source of life to energize the community to perform this mission. The Spirit, through whom Jesus is present in the community, abides with all disciples, bringing peace, joy, a sense of unity, reconciliation, understanding of the truth, and prophetic challenge to the world. Because of this life-giving presence, the Spirit-Paraclete is creative of community. Because of the presence of the comforter, the entire community—and each person within the community—is capable of greater things than they ever dared hope or imagine. And because of the presence of the Comforter—the strengthening, enlivening, animating presence of the Comforter—the community, and each member of the community, is called to bring that vision of new possibilities to life within a greater world.

Mary as Disciple: The Johannine Portrait

Sometime before the turn of the first century CE,[20] an unknown member of an early Christian community wrote what we now call the fourth gospel or the gospel of John. This author lived and wrote in a Jewish world shaped by the Old Testament and especially steeped in Isaian and Wisdom traditions.[21] Scholars agree that a major Johannine theme emerged out of the Jewish Christian conflicts of the times. Christians had been expelled from their own Jewish synagogues and urgently needed to find viable alternatives for the religious structures and viewpoints of Judaism. The depth of their emotion as they attempted to deal with that separation still permeates the text of John's gospel.

This faithful Jewish community was also shaken by the death of the "Beloved Disciple." He had been their preeminent authority, their direct link to Jesus. We no longer know just who this Beloved Disciple was, but whoever the Beloved One had been, he was now gone. His community had felt especially privileged by his presence and witness. Because of him they considered themselves closer to the historical Jesus and more in tune with his true message than were the communities whose connection to Jesus came through Peter and the twelve.[22] Preserving this distinctive heritage, in fact, provided further impetus for the evangelist to record his community's reflections on the import of Jesus for their own lives and for an even more universal audience.

That the anonymous Beloved Disciple, rather than Peter and the twelve, established the Johannine community's credibility is important to us because it has significant consequences for the future of discipleship. At a time when apostles were taking on increasing importance in the memory of other Christian communities and a variety of "orders" were taking shape, discipleship was the "primary Christian category" for John. The fourth gospel reveres all disciples and presents the Beloved Disciple as a paradigm for their discipleship. For the Johannine author, what was paramount was following Jesus and being obedient to his word—being disciple. When this author uses the term "apostle" at all, it is never in the technical sense of the Synoptics, but rather in the spirit of the Wisdom tradition, where it refers to an envoy or messenger, one sent on a mission.[23] In John's gospel, that role belongs to women, as well as to men, to an extraordinary degree.

Elisabeth Fiorenza comments on the astonishing prominence accorded women in the narrative:

> S/he begins and ends Jesus' public ministry with a story about a woman, Mary, the mother of Jesus, and Mary of Bethany. Alongside the Pharisee Nicodemus s/he places the Samaritan woman; alongside the Christological confession of Peter s/he places that of Martha. Four women and the beloved disciple stand beneath the cross of Jesus. Mary of Magdala is not only the first to witness the empty tomb but also the first to receive an appearance of the resurrected Lord. Thus at crucial points of the narrative, *women emerge as exemplary disciples and apostolic witnesses.*[24]

It is within this milieu of "discipleship of equals," to use Fiorenza's descriptive phrase, that Mary of Nazareth assumes a most significant role of disciple.

Mary of Nazareth appears on two highly significant and interconnected Johannine narratives that inaugurate and conclude Jesus' mission on earth—the wedding feast at Cana and the Crucifixion. Both events are crucial to the gospel's Christology, making radical turning points in Jesus' mission; in each he is changed and takes on a new life. In addition to establishing his primary Christological concern, however, the evangelist also wished to highlight the presence of Mary. According to a noted ecumenical study of Mary's role in scripture,

> The very fact that the mother of Jesus is mentioned in the first verse, which supplies the setting for the scene, and that she raises the question concerning the wine, clearly directs the reader's attention to her and her expectations.[25]

Study of the Cana story's origins shed further light on the significance of Mary's role. Scholars generally accept Fortna's theory that the Johannine author based his account on a story circulating at that time about Jesus' life previous to his public ministry. Here is Raymond Brown's translation of the Fortna reconstruction of the original story:

> Now there was a wedding at Cana of Galilee, and the
> mother of Jesus was there. Jesus himself and his disciples
> had been invited to the wedding celebration. But they had
> no wine, for the wine provided for the wedding banquet had
> been used up. The mother of Jesus told the waiters: "Do
> whatever he tells you." There were at hand six stone water
> jars, each holding fifteen to twenty-five gallons. "Fill those
> jars with water," Jesus ordered. . . . [26]

In this version, Mary appears as a person who believed in Jesus, at least
as a wonder worker, a view John considers a clear misunderstanding of
Jesus. When John used this story to begin the first part of his gospel, he
made two important modifications: first, he added an introductory
phrase, "on the third day," and then he inserted a key dialog between
Jesus and Mary right at the heart of the story. What can this entire
narrative and, in particular, its Johannine additions, tell us about the
role of Mary in the fourth gospel?

Mary appears only twice in John's gospel—at Cana and Calvary, the
first and final signs of Jesus. The evangelist immediately gives us clues
to the relationship of these two encounters by coloring the Cana narrative to evoke the messianic age. He begins: "On the third day." John's
audience was well aware that Christ's glory is manifested and God's
people are saved "on the third day," so they are alert to a message about
their salvation. John later reinforces his point by stressing Jesus'
"hour," a key term the evangelist uses *only* for Jesus' moment of
exaltation or "lifting up"—his death, resurrection, and glory. (It is
unique to John's gospel that this entire event occurs at Calvary.) By
using both "on the third day" and Jesus' "hour," John forged an intimate
link for his audience between the events of Cana and the central event at
Calvary.[27] The "hour" of Cana reaches its fullness in the final "hour" of
Calvary; at that critical moment we shall see that Jesus' "hour" is also to
be the "hour" of Mary.

A wedding banquet with abundant wine is a strong motif in the
Wisdom tradition and in John's gospel. In Proverbs, Lady Wisdom pre-
pares a banquet to which she invites her followers (9:2-6). By eating her
meal and drinking her wine, her disciples symbolize their acceptance of
her teaching. The Johannine Jesus had already been introduced as
Word-Wisdom in the prolong. Now, at a banquet in Cana, Jesus who is

Divine Wisdom gives his disciples abundant wine to drink, and his followers come to believe in him.

> The miracle of Cana is a sign that Jesus is the true Wisdom
> offering the wine of his revelation in place of the water of
> Torah. . . . Jesus performs the Cana miracle in the pres-
> ence of his disciples, and they believe in him, offering him
> the allegiance which Wisdom demanded of her followers.[28]

When one considers the dialog in the Johannine Cana account, it certainly seems odd, if not impertinent, for Jesus to address his mother as "woman," not only there, but also on Calvary. No known precedent exists in either Hebrew or Greek culture. However, since Jesus also addresses the Samaritan woman, the woman caught in adultery, and Mary of Magdala as "woman," the term can hardly be considered disrespectful. Rather, according to Fiorenza, it places Mary of Nazareth in the category of women who were "apostolic witnesses and exemplary disciples."[29]

The interpolated dialog is quite likely John's version of the Synoptics' accounts rejecting physical relationship as a criterion for discipleship. On the other hand, as René Laurentin points out, Mary's mediation was *not* rejected by Jesus. The pattern of rebuff and persistence is, in fact, characteristic of John's gospel. All three major sections begin with two episodes of direct mediation by a woman to which Jesus responds with a salvific sign:

> Women have a role which is not only active and dynamic
> but anticipatory, with reference to the faith. . . . (They
> display) an initiative and creativity which forestall, not only
> the other disciples, but Jesus himself. He seems to be aston-
> ished by these anticipations.[30]

In each case, Jesus' response to a woman's persistence is positive. Johannine discipleship is a far cry from the passive servitude that we sometimes read back into the gospels!

When Mary of Nazareth directs the servants, "Do whatever he tells you," she initiates the series of encounters wherein the evangelist shows how people come to Christian belief: faith in Jesus comes to people through the mediation of disciples. Mary's words are addressed to the *diokonoi* (servants). The Johannine community used this term to describe those who served at table or, as we would put it today, presided at the eucharistic celebration. When John's audience heard this story, then, they understood Mary's admonition was not addressed to an anonymous band of waiters but to all Christian disciples.

In the Synoptics, Jesus asserts that his disciples are those who hear his word and do it. The first four chapters of John also make clear that true faith is based on accepting the word of Jesus. Now, at Cana, it is Mary who calls the *diakonoi*/disciples to do the word of the Lord, and we are told that "only they knew" the sign was from Jesus. We discover in this Johannine dialog a significant intermediary role for Mary in the Christian community. She presents people's needs to Jesus and she calls them to true discipleship: hearing the word and doing it. Mary has begun her role of mediating salvation—the journey of faith that will climax at Calvary when she is joined with Jesus' true family in faith. Mediating salvation, as we saw, is what Isaiah meant by the term "Comforter of the Afflicted." Mary appears at Cana as one who will usher in God's new world of loving justice.

Mary makes her second and final appearance in the fourth gospel as Jesus is raised on the cross. Once again she is present at a radical turning point in Jesus' life. His mission on earth is almost completed. He is to take on a new life. Here, as at Cana, the evangelist's primary Christological concern is joined to a clear effort to highlight the presence of Mary of Nazareth. The Johannine author establishes Mary's centrality in this scene by employing a common Hebrew literary device, the chiastic pattern, in which related episodes are arranged symmetrically in a series of inverted parallels. The significance of each episode is highlighted by reflecting on its parallel text, and the central episode in the chiastic structure holds the key to understanding the writer's primary intent. Brown's structural analysis of the crucifixion scene shows Mary is present at the pivotal point in the narrative:

INTRODUCTION: Jesus raised on cross (19:16b-18)

    A   Inscription: "Jesus, King of the Jews"
              Pilate denies Jews' request (19:19-22)

        B   The seamless tunic (19:23-24)
                  Jesus' clothes divided.

            | C   Woman and Beloved Disciple (19:25-27) |

        B^1 Jesus thirsts, sips wine (19:28-30)
                Jesus hands over his spirit

    A^1 Pilate agrees on Jews' request (19:31-37)
              Blood and water pour forth (the spirit)

CONCLUSION: Jesus taken down from cross and buried (19:38-52)

Here, at the climactic centerpiece of the gospel narrative, which the evangelist presents as Jesus' "hour" of triumph, Mary's function has changed drastically from the inaugural role she assumed at Cana. At this crucial moment, attention is focused on Jesus' concern for the future welfare of "his own" for whom he desires to show his great love in "the hour" of his departure. By placing Mary at the heart of this scene, the author deliberately casts her in the context of discipleship, establishing her central role in the future of the community of believers.[31]

In the Wisdom tradition, "behold" is a technical term. It is followed immediately by God's message describing the person's unique mission and significance (as, for instance, "Behold the lamb of God who takes away the sin of the world"). In each case, the announcement makes the hearer take a second look. This person is special. There is more to her or him than meets the eye.[32] S/he has a special mission from God.

Like Mary, addressed as "woman" from Calvary, the Beloved Disciple also remains nameless; this disciple is every Christian. Although both of them are real people, their anonymity establishes John's primary interest in their symbolic importance. The words "Behold your son" and "Behold your mother" not only establish the mission of these two central figures, but also reveal the deep spiritual relationship that was to exist between them.

Commenting on the significance of that relationship, the ecumenical Marian taskforce concluded:

> In giving the beloved disciple to Mary as her son, and Mary to the disciple as his mother, Jesus brought into existence a new community of believing disciples, the same "eschatological family" which appears in the synoptic gospels . . .
> Mary, who in the Cana episode had been distinguished from the disciples, now becomes the mother of the disciple *par excellence*, and so becomes herself a model of belief and discipleship.[33]

The words, "Behold your son" and "Behold your mother," not only establish the favorable light in which John now casts Mary but also stand in remarkable contrast to his harsh portrayal of the brothers as total unbelievers (John 7:6-8), who have no place in Jesus' new family of disciples.

The Johannine author concludes the scene with the significant statement, "After this, aware that all was now finished, he handed over his spirit" (19:30). In using the expression "after this," the evangelist indicates that the missioning of the Mother and the Son is explicitly connected to completion of Jesus' mission on earth and the handing over of his spirit. Jesus leaves behind a small community of believers to carry on his mission. His dying breath symbolizes the passing on of his life—the spirit of comfort, the other Paraclete he had promised his friends at the Last Supper. In the moment of Jesus' death, the community of disciples is born. Jesus has proclaimed Mary, Mother of Disciples, all enlivened by the spirit of Jesus. The nurturing, mothering love of the Spirit of God is embodied in Mary in a special way. Mary's Johannine community thus provides significant theological roots for her later emergence as the feminine face of God.

Some Conclusions and Questions

What is the significance for a feminist considering Mary under the title of "Comforter of the Afflicted"? Historically, of course, the route tracing backward from the Litany of Loretto to the Isaian Servant who comforts Yahweh's people is intangible. The fact remains, however, that this title has been applied to Mary at least as far back as the oral roots of the litany and, in variations of the title, reaches back to the patristic period. The title, then, has colored our perception of Mary and her role in Christian life. It reflects a theology of Mary that found its way into popular religion—has generally been taken to include all of those qualities that "Comforter of the Afflicted" psychologists would describe as "nurturing qualities": listening, sympathizing, caring, attending. It describes those occupations deemed suitable for women: nursing, child-nurturing, homemaking, consoling the bereaved, feeding the hungry, sheltering the homeless. . . .

When we turn to the Isaian roots of "Comforter," we find a continuity with these concepts. First of all, this title is uniquely true of God's relationship to humanity—a relationship often described in feminine terms. This "feminine face of God" becomes the core of the prophetic vocation in Deutero Isaiah: to be a prophet *is* to comfort the afflicted—to follow, so to speak, in God's footsteps!

How the prophet comforts the afflicted, however, is much more dynamic and radical in Deutero Isaiah than it is in the present popular perception. For Deutero Isaiah "to comfort" is synonymous with "to bring salvation." In other words, the prophetic goal is to usher in God's peaceable kingdom of love and peace, truth and justice. The prophet comforts by seeing her world with God's loving vision, by radically confronting all that is out of kilter in her world, and by proclaiming new possibilities for life and freedom. The prophet knows that true comfort comes only when people are free from all that is oppressive in their lives.

What I am saying about the role of prophet is nothing new, certainly. Realizing that "Comforter of the Afflicted" refers to this radical prophetic role is quite another matter, however. Christian feminists might gain provocative insights by reflecting on the intrinsic equation Second Isaiah makes between women's traditional (and supposedly passive) tasks of nurturing or comforting and the absolute necessity for radical confrontation with that which oppresses the comfortless.

Throughout much of history, the task of one-on-one nurturing has been systematically dichotomized from what I call "nurturing in the public sector," that is, engaging with others in united efforts to alleviate systemic oppression. Women were relegated to exclusively privatized roles, while men were sole proprietors of the public sector. Second Isaiah's image of Comforter can provide a strong symbol for Christian feminists intent on reclaiming the necessary and integral connection between private and public nurturing. The vision of discipleship embodied in the title, "Comforter of the Afflicted," calls us to inquire: What are the prophetic dimensions of my ministry? If my work is in a church-related institution, do I give visible witness against the church's injustice to women? Are my visits to the sick and elderly linked to political efforts for nursing home reform and more adequate social security system? Are my efforts to establish a food pantry or soup kitchen matched by my efforts to end unemployment and to divert the massive flow of funds from armaments to human needs?

What is freedom for the people to whom I minister? How can their oppression be alleviated? These are the hard questions we must face and the criterion we must use to establish priorities in our ministry—if, that is, we choose to make the biblical vision of Comforter normative for our ministry. May Mary, Comforter of the Afflicted, Mother of the community of disciples, help us find ways to minister more authentically in the prophetic tradition enlivened by the comforting Spirit of God.

Footnotes

1   Elisabeth Schu³ssler Fiorenza, *In Memory of Her: A Feminist Theological Reconstruction of Christian Origins* (Crossroad, 1983), p. 33. Fiorenza suggests that feminist theology requires a paradigm that understands the New Testament as a prototype rather than an archetype. Unlike archtypes, which are unchanging ideal models, prototypes allow for variation from the original and are thus "critically open to the possibility" of being transformed.

2   Whatever is said of Mary's role in the gospels, then, is always referring to Luke's interpretation or John's interpretation and in no way imputes characteristic virtues (or vices) to Mary, the historical mother of Jesus. This does not imply that all the Marian narratives are purely the product of the evangelists' imaginations. Rather, it respects their intent in writing which was theological reflection on the meaning of Christian life in their own early communities. In other words, our questions are often simply not the same as the evangelists' questions.

3   My opinion here is partially based on my acceptance of a major contention in *Mary in the New Testament*: Mary "did not follow Jesus as a disciple during the ministry" but she did share "the faith in Jesus of the earliest Christian community" from the first (John 19; Acts 1:14, 2:1). Raymond E. Brown, Karl P. Donfried, Joseph A. Fitzmyer, and John Reumann (eds.) (Fortress Press and Paulist Press, 1978), p. 284.

4   Richard J. Dillon, "Retrospect in the Cana Account (John 2:1-11)," (*Catholic Biblical Quarterly*, Vol. 24), p. 278, and Brown, *Mary*, p. 143

5   Rosemary Radford Ruether, *Mary—the Feminine Face of the Church* (Westminster Press, 1977), *passim*, and *New Woman/New Earth* (Seabury, 1975) pp. 50-53; Marina Warner, *Alone of All Her Sex: The Myth and Cult of the Virgin Mary* (Knopf, 1976), *passim*

6   The term "prophet servant" is used following the explanation of Gerhard Von Rad in *The Message of the Prophets* (Harper and Row, 1965) pp. 221, 225

7   Cf. Raymond Brown, "The Paraclete," Appendix V in Anchor Bible Commentary 29A, *The Gospel According to John XIII-XXI*, pp. 1135-1143

8   Otto Schmitz-Gustav Stahlin, "Comfort and Comfortlessness in the O.T.," in Gerhard Kittel, *Theological Dictionary of the New Testament*, Vol. V (Wm. B. Eerdman, 1964) p. 789

9   In her significant new book, *In Memory of Her*, Fiorenza warns against prooftexting or ignoring the basic partriarchal bias of scripture and calls for a "hermeneutic of suspicion." I find her cautions helpful and, while not pretending to have heeded her warnings as fully as I might wish, hope a study of Second Isaiah's "Comforter" meets some of her guidelines (pp. 56, 108).

10 Translated from the Hebrew *nacham*; in the Greek of the Septuagint, *parakletos* (in Latin, *Consolator* or *Advocatus*)

11 H. Riesenfeld, "A Probable Background to the Johannine Paraclete," *Studies in the History of Religion* (Leiden: Brill, 1972) p. 268 passim; O. Schmitz, "Parakaleo and Paraklesis in the N.T.," in Kittle, *Theological Dictionary*, Vol. V, p. 799; J.G. Davies, "The Primary Meaning of Paraclete," *Journal of Theological Studies:* New Series iv, Part 1 (April, 1953) pp. 35-38; George Johnston, *The Spirit Paraclete in the Gospel of John* (Cambridge Univ. Press, 1970) p. 74

12 Phyllis Trible, *God and the Rhetoric of Sexuality* (Fortress Press, 1978), pp. 38-52, quote p. 33. See also Leonard Swidler, *Biblical Affirmations of Woman* (Westminster Press, 1979), pp. 31-34; Yves Congar, "The Spirit as God's Femininity" condensed in *Theology Digest* (Vol. 30, No. 2, 1982) p. 129. Other Isaian references to God as a mother who comforts include Isaiah 42:13, 14; 46:3, 4; 66:12, 13

13 José Miranda, *Marx and the Bible*, trans. J. Eagleson (Orbis, 1974) pp. 46, 47, 85

14 Riesenfeld, pp. 269-72

15 See especially Edward Schillebeeckx, *Jesus: An Experiment in Christology* (1974, English translation: *Seabury Press,* c1979); pp. 48 passim, 488-49. Also Walter Brueggemann, *In Man We Trust: The Neglected Side of Biblical Faith* (John Knox Press, 1972); M. Jack Suggs, *Wisdom, Christology, and Law in Matthew's Gospel* (Harvard University Press, 1970); Raymond E. Brown, *The Gospel According to John I-XII* (Anchor Bible Vol. 29, Doubleday, 1966), pp. lii-lxiv, cxxii-cxxv

16 Robert Kysar, *The Fourth Evangelist and His Gospel: An Examination of Contemporary Scholarship* (Augsburg Pub., 1975), p. 19

17 Bruce Vawter, "John's Doctrine of the Spirit: A Summary of His Eschatology," in *A Companion to John: Readings in Johannine Theology* ed. by Michael Taylor, SJ, p. 179 (Alba House, 1977)

18   Hans Windisch, *The Spirit-Paraclete in the Fourth Gospel* (Fortress Press, 1968, first published 1927), p. 11

19   D. Moody Smith, *John* Proclamation Commentaries: The New Testament Witness for Preaching, Gerhard Krodel, ed. (Fortress Press, 1976)

20   Kysar, p. 166ff. Reporting on current scholarship in the field, Kysar explains that later datings were revised when the Roberts' fragment of the gospel was discovered. Scholars agree it was circulating in Egypt at the time to which it is dated, 135-150 CE. Most Johannine scholars now place the date of composition between 80 and 90 "but a surprisingly strong movement toward pushing the date of the gospel back before 70 is detected." Some even argue for the late '50s or early '60s, but haven't gained much scholarly acceptance. Nevertheless, present research does reject a late dating and opens the door to the possibility of an earlier dating.

21   Kysar, p. 170

22   Fiorenza, p. 326

23   Kysar, p. 165

24   John uses the Greek verbs "to send" *(apostellein, pempein)* so often that scholars are concluding the term describes the very nature and mission of Jesus. He is the messenger from God, the one sent. In Jesus' post-Resurrection appearances to the disciples, he says to them: "As the Father has sent me, so I am sending you" (John 20:21). It is interesting to note that the same verb, *send (apostellein)* is used in 4:38 to describe the missionary role of the Samaritan woman who is sent to reap fields ripe for the harvest. That is clearly "missionary language." Kysar, p. 195; Brown, *Mary,* pp. 690-91.

25   Fiorenza, p. 326

26   Brown, *Mary,* p. 187

27   Brown, *Gospel,* Vol. 29, pp. 517-18. Brown lists and comments on the 26 uses of "hour" in the fourth gospel.

28   Dillon, pp. 287-88. Rudolf Schnackenburg, *The Gospel According to St. John,* Vol. I (Herder, 1968), pp. 338-39. Schnackenburg, for one, disagrees with this interpretation of Jesus as Wisdom. I believe, however, that today's scholars are growing increasingly convinced of the profound (though hitherto largely ignored) influence of Wisdom traditions throughout the gospels.

29   Fiorenza, p. 326

30   René Laurentin, "Jesus and Woman: An Underestimated Revolution," pp. 82-92 in *Women in a Men's Church* ed. by Virgil Elizondo and Norbert Greinacher, (Seabury Press, 1980), p. 86

31   Brown, *Mary,* pp. 206, 212; Brown, *Gospel,* Vol. 29A, pp. 912-13

32   Brown, *Mary,* p. 212ff

33   *Ibid.,* pp. 288-89

MARY, MIRROR OF JUSTICE: A CHALLENGE FOR THE CHURCH TO REFLECT JUSTICE
Mary Donahey, BVM

In praying the Litany of Our Lady of Loretto, the church explicitly acknowledges Mary as "Mirror of Justice." The theology of that same church considers Mary as a type of the church. For example, theologian Richard McBrien wrote, Mary "is an image, a model, a figure, or a *type* of the church and of Christian existence."[1] In this theology, therefore, Mary can bridge our understanding of the church and our understanding of Christian existence. That is, Mary bridges our understanding of the church and our understanding of Christian ethics and Christian spirituality. Elsewhere, McBrien noted that to study Mary is to study the intersection of distinctive Catholic values or the theological principles of mediation, communion, and sacramentality. In the principles of mediation and sacramentality, the Catholic tradition insists "that the invisible God is present and available in the visible, the finite, the historical, the concrete, the tangible, the fleshly." In the principle of communion, we discover that the "effect of the divine work is ultimately the unification of the human community and of the whole of creation . . . Mary is at once the bearer of God (sacramentality), a principal collaborator in redemption (mediation), and the primary member of the church (communion)."[2]

So when our piety and our theology laud Mary as "Mirror of Justice," we are, at least, implicitly recognizing that the rest of the church is to mirror justice as this primary member does. This goal was included in the 1971 World Synod of Bishops' proclamation that "Action on behalf of *justice* and participation in the transformation of the world fully appear to us as a constitutive dimension of the preaching of the gospel, or, in other words, of the church's mission for the redemption of the human race and its liberation from every oppressive situation."[3] The full preaching of the gospel thus involves the church in *action on behalf of justice*, action to liberate people from "every oppressive situation."

But what is this justice that is mirrored by Mary and that is to be reflected in the church? Presumably, Mary's understanding and expression of justice grew out of the Old Testament insights into justice. Her people, after all, covenanted with a God who strove to form and reform a community characterized by justice or grounded in justice.

Old Testament Understanding of Justice

The earliest Old Testament discussion of the justice of God occurs on the occasion of Abraham's intercession for Sodom (Genesis 18:17-33). José Miranda saw this passage as the key to the Yahwistic theology of the first four books of the Bible. (The Yahwist, in the cosmopolitan time of David, may have used the theme of justice as a principle of selection when sorting through the Abrahamic traditions.) That Genesis passage tells how to keep the way of the Lord:

> The Lord said . . . that Abraham shall become a great and mighty nation, and all the nations of the earth shall bless themselves by him . . . I have chosen him, that he may charge his children and his household after him to keep the way of the Lord by doing righteousness and justice; so that the Lord may bring to Abraham what he has promised him (Genesis 18:17-19).

The oldest scriptural authors wrote to affirm that doing justice "was *the* purpose of Yahweh's intervention in human history."[4] Thirty more times, the Old Testament used that phrase, "righteousness and justice" (or "justice and righteousness"), to signify social justice—justice for the poor, oppressed, and needy.

After escaping from oppressive conditions in Egypt, Israel set forth her sense of justice in the ordinances Moses passed on to the people from the Lord. In Exodus 23:1-9, we see that

　　1. A just community was to have due process of the law.

"You shall not utter a false report" nor be a malicious
witness, nor take a bribe, "for a bribe blinds the officials,
and subverts the cause of those who are in the right."
"You shall not pervert the justice due to your poor in his
suit."

2. Biblical justice extends to helping one's enemy.
"If you meet your enemy's ox or his ass going astray, you
shall bring it back to him. If you see the ass of one who
hates you lying under its burden, you shall refrain from
leaving him with it, you shall help him to lift it up."

3. In scriptural justice, there is a perception of common
humanity.
"You shall not oppress a stranger; you know the heart of
a stranger, for you were strangers in the land of Egypt."

The primary form of distributive justice in the Bible is according to
one's need. This went hand in hand with the scriptural maxim to
contribute according to one's ability:

If there is among you a poor man, one of your brethren, in
any of your towns within your land which the Lord your
God gives you, you shall not harden your heart or shut your
hand against your poor brother, but you shall open your
hand to him, and lend him sufficient for his need, whatever
it may be . . . You shall open wide your hand to your
brother, to the needy and to the poor, in the land (Deuteronomy 15:7-11).

The first concern, then, in distributing the goods of society is to help the
least advantaged. It is, after all, from their position that a social system
is judged.

The God revealed in the history of Mary's people was a God who
"executes justice for the fatherless and the widow, and loves the
sojourner, giving the sojourner food and clothing. Love the sojourner
therefore; for you were sojourners in the land of Egypt" (Deuteronomy
10:18-19; Exodus 22:21-22). It is because of this love that justice is
the equal treatment of all human beings solely on the
grounds that as human they are bestowed worth by God.
The command of justice to God's people was based on what
they had received in the gracious acts of God . . . Since

their lives are founded on God's grace rather than on their
merit, and since they see that others are in the same position of need, it is need which determines the distribution of
justice rather than worth, birth, merit, or ability. It is the
assumption that all have equal merit which allows justice to
be expressed by the principle of equality. Otherwise, egalitarian treatment would be an expression of benevolence
over and beyond what people are owed in justice.[5]

An outstanding ideal of biblical justice was the Year of Jubilee,
which was to be celebrated every 50 years. If a poor person must sell his
property, "then what he sold shall remain in the hand of him who
bought it until the year of jubilee; in the jubilee it shall be released, and
he shall return to his property" (Leviticus 25:28). Thus, twice every
century, foreclosed land was to be returned to the family whose heritage
it was. This redistributionary process gave everyone access to land from
which to produce a living. Such a law prevented the concentration of
power and wealth in the hands of a few. Israelite society, therefore, was
not to be partitioned into the extravagantly rich and the deprived poor.

There was also the sabbatical year, or a year of release. "At the end of
every seven years you shall grant a release . . . Every creditor shall
release what he has lent to his neighbor . . . There will be no poor
among you" (Deuteronomy 15:1-4). "For six years you shall sow your
land and gather in its yield; but the seventh year you shall let it rest and
lie fallow, that the poor of your people may eat . . . You shall do
likewise with your vineyard, and with your olive orchard" (Exodus
23:10-11; Leviticus 25:3f). This practice combatted poverty which
ruined the poor (Proverbs 10:15).

Justice was a strong theme in the history of Mary's people even
before the entry of the classical prophets, who, however, sharpened the
focus of that justice. They knew that only false prophets promised
personal salvation apart from social justice. Amos was experiencing the
peasants' loss of economic and social place in the northern Kingdom of
Israel. He excoriated the merchants who could hardly wait for the holy
days to pass so they could get back to their fraudulent practices:

Hear this, you who trample upon the needy, and bring the
poor of the land to an end, saying, "When will the new
moon be over, that we may sell grain? And the sabbath, that

we may offer wheat for sale, that we may make the ephah small and the shekel great, and deal deceitfully with false balances, that we may buy the poor for silver and the needy for a pair of sandals, and sell the refuse of the wheat?" (Amos 8:4-6)

True worship was not the feast, solemn assemblies, burnt offerings, cereal offerings, peace offerings, noisy songs, melodious harps, but "justice roll[ing] down like waters and righteousness like an ever-flowing stream" (Amos 5:24). Prophetic justice does not rest until the poor gain independence by sharing power in the community. Amos's denunciation of Israel and her neighbors for reliance upon militarism and for social injustice, and his criticism of empty piety and religious authorities did not go unnoticed by those civil and religious authorities whose power was threatened. Amaziah, the priest of Bethel, told Amos to return to Judah and "never again prophesy at Bethel, for it is the King's sanctuary, and it is a temple of the kingdom" (Amos 7:13).

By the time of Isaiah's eighth-century song or allegory of the vineyard, an aristocracy had taken over the peasant holdings in Judah. So Isaiah describes the Lord's judgment on the elders (the primary administrators of justice) and on the princes (the royal appointees): "It is you who have devoured the vineyard, the spoil of the poor is in your houses. What do you mean by crushing my people, by grinding the face of the poor?' says the Lord God of hosts" (Isaiah 3:14-15). The women in Jerusalem who have profited by such corruption will be smitten with a scab and their secret parts laid bare. Their finery will be taken away (Isaiah 3:17f). The Lord "looked for justice, but behold, bloodshed . . . Woe to those who join house to house, who add field to field until there is no more room and you are made to dwell alone in the midst of the land" (Isaiah 5:7-8).

In Second Isaiah's First Servant Song, God is portrayed as putting his Spirit upon his servant who "will bring forth justice to the nations . . . He will not fail or be discouraged till he has established justice in the earth" (Isaiah 42:1-4). "The servant (Israel in exile) was given the task of establishing the just order of life which will prevail for all peoples when God extends his rule universally."[6]

Third Isaiah, the theologian(s) of the post-exile period, begins his preaching: "Thus says the Lord: 'Keep justice, and do righteousness' "

(Isaiah 56:1). Like Amos 5:24, this Isaiah knew that fasting was not humbling oneself, bowing one's head, spreading sackcloth and ashes under one, but loosening the bonds of wickedness, undoing the thongs of the yoke, letting the oppressed go free, breaking every yoke, sharing bread with the hungry, bringing the homeless poor into one's house, covering the naked and not hiding oneself from one's own flesh (Isaiah 58:5-7).

These scriptural passages give some of the strength of Israel's passion for justice. Hebrew justice was not an other-worldly justice, but one worked out in history. Israel was aware of "the evils which destroy the social fabric of society," and her God was "compassionate to the oppressed and vindicator of the poor."[8]

In the post-exilic intertestamental period, Judaism emphasized the justice of the individual. This individualizing of justice was triggered by the codification in book form of the Psalms, which could then be used by individuals. At the same time, Judaism became more sectarian as it identified the just individual with one who avoided Hellenization and religious syncretism. Another transformation of justice was that it was now expected that God's justice will be made evident only at the end of time. And, lastly, Judaism identified justice with almsgiving or care for the poor. To be charitable and concerned for the neighbor is to be just. "Concern for the poor and a desire to lessen the inequality between rich and poor either individually or collectively, in a biblical perspective . . . is rooted in claims of justice, i.e., how one can be faithful to the Lord who has given the goods of the earth as *common* possession of all and be faithful to others in the human community who have equal claim to these goods."[9]

Mary's Understanding of Justice

This desire to lessen the inequality between rich and poor appears to throb in Mary's heart, for she enters the New Testament scene proclaiming a Magnificat laden with justice implications. In the eyes of the early church, who was this Mary? Luke chose to write about her according to the model of Hannah.

In the song of Hannah, the view of the Lord as the great equalizer is present: "He raises up the poor from the dust; he lifts the needy from the ash heap, to make them sit with princes and inherit a seat of honor" (I Samuel 2:8; also Psalm 113:7-9). As Hannah knew, those who have created the oppressive structures that produce distress will in God's time have their fortunes reversed: "The bows of the mighty are broken . . . Those who were full have hired themselves out for bread . . . she who has many children is forlorn" (I Samuel 2:4-5).

Being modeled after the Bible's "most faithful and loyal mother,"[10] Mary responded to Gabriel by identifying herself as the servant of the Lord. Hannah, too, had frequently referred to herself as handmaid of the Lord (I Samuel 1:11, 16, 18).

Like Hannah (and Judith, the "Jewess" who personifies oppressed Judaism[11]), Mary speaks for the Anawim, the antithesis of the proud. Mary sings a song of the oppressed and weak people (I Samuel 1:11, 2:1-10; Judith 13:18, 16:11). Speaking of God as her savior (Luke 1:47), Mary turns back salvation from being associated with Jesus' death and resurrection to being associated with his birth. Mary received the revelation that "the Anawim encountered salvation when they proclaimed Jesus as the Messiah."[12]

Mary's Magnificat contains the theme of joy, developed by Luke in the rest of his gospel. Mary's "spirit finds joy in God" her savior (1:47), the Baptist leapt for joy in Elizabeth's womb (1:44), the disciples were to rejoice that their "names are inscribed in heaven" (10:20), and "Jesus rejoiced in the Holy Spirit" (10:21).

No doubt this theme of joy is related to the Magnificat's core theme— the reversal of destiny for the lowly and hungry. To try to save the proud, the strong, the wealthy and to exalt the lowly and give "every good thing" to the hungry, God (or God's order) brings inner confusion to the proud, dethrones the mighty, sends the rich "empty away" (1:51-53).

In these lines of the canticle attributed to Mary, the Latin American theologian, Arturo Paoli saw a résumé of the Bible. Contending that the leading idea of Luke's gospel is God deposing the mighty, raising up the lowly, giving the hungry every good thing, and sending the rich empty away, Paoli said:

> We are left perplexed by the thought that the church
> declares Mary to be its model, wishing to reproduce her in

its life-style, and yet the church that people see the most of
and talk most about is on the side of the "mighty" whom
God means to depose and the "proud" whom God means
to confuse. But here and there signs appear, little breakthroughs of a hidden church within the church, like the
luscious fruit inside a rind that is much too thick. These
breakthoughs are enough to give me hope and the courage
needed to continue the struggle for the entry of the whole
church into the perspective of Mary.[13]

In Paoli's meditation or critique, the majority of church leaders are
not yet into the perspective of Mary. It was not a queen, but a poor,
perhaps unlettered woman whom God led to discover the mercy that
bridges generations. Remaking itself in the image of Mary, the church
would discover that partiality to the poor becomes universality ("global-
ity") and that real goodness arises only from this option for the poor.
Such coherence, Paoli believed, would produce effective denunciations
and strong compassion.

The reason the situation in Latin America is so sacrilegious, according to Paoli, is that the gospel of Christ is used to cloak injustice.
Bolivian workers stave off hunger by chewing coca leaves; the poor of
Northeastern Brazil eat worms from the infested puddles of slum alley-
ways. These poor are not coming from a Provident Father who gives
every good thing to the hungry; they are coming from unjust property
arrangements.

Paoli saw the poor discovering the Lucan image of Mary, an image
that contributes to true human dignity. Mary inspires the poor to aim
toward "bread, work, housing, schooling, a share in the decision-
making process, equal rights. Thus one would feel truly a person and
would enjoy here on earth the pleasure and happiness that Christ
proclaimed and intended for all."[14]

The Magnificat's paradox of joy and pain is continued in the bloody
struggle for justice, for the defense of people's right to essential goods.
Every generation must gain its right to happiness in a context of
conflict and pain.

In the jails and martyrdoms of today, Paoli sees the birth of the new
Christian who defends the neighbor. These are the real change-agents,
the martyrs. They have discovered that to suffer for others is probably

the only purpose in life. It is the source of a joy surpassing the most jubilant worldly celebration because the person who lays down his/her life for others is reborn into a previously unknown brotherhood and sisterhood—a relation of love.

> [If] we have not felt ourselves in love with everything in such a way that nothing remains apart—separated—from us, we shall not be able to resist the waves of history . . . The greater the vigor with which the projects of the proud—their insolent power, the security established by despising others—are resisted, the clearer will be the victory.
>
> The song of Mary proclaims the terrible judgment of the dispossessed, the true and great victory of poverty, of weakness, of the Cross.[15]

Simeon had warned that the sword of division would pierce Mary's soul (Luke 2:35). "Every person must face the sword of deciding what doing the word of God means, a sword that divides the believer from the non-believer."[16]

Pierced by a sword thrust out from an unjust world, Mary suffered what for many of us is "the worst we can imagine,"[17] the ignominious death of one's innocent child. Victimized by such injustice, Mary is a ready symbol to which others may relate who, too, must pass through inconsolable grief and continue the struggle for what is right and decent in this world. She raised a son who was an equalizer. The effectiveness of his "last-shall-be-first" sentiments threatened the political and religious order. Hence, he was crucified. It is no accident that "Mary the mother of Jesus" (Acts 1:14) was present in that Jerusalem upstairs room as the community was formed to continue the ideals for which Jesus went to his death. No doubt her guiding hand and wisdom were as influential in mothering this communal body as they were in nurturing the world's savior.

For the downtrodden, Mary can be a mirror of identity—one in whom they see themselves. She can also be a symbol of their survival. The oppressed can find hope in devotion to the Mary they meet in the Christian gospel. Like them, this Mary is of low estate.

In the Lucan Beatitudes, Jesus says "Blest are you poor . . . Blest are you who hunger . . . But woe to you rich . . . Woe to you who are full" (Luke 6:20-25). This merely repeats the Magnificat's God putting down the mighty, sending the rich away empty, exalting the lowly, filling the hungry. Gospel devotion to Mary and her son cannot be cut loose from its moorings in social concern—concern for the economically poor and oppressed. Luke presents Mary as the first and most perfect of Christ's disciples "because she understood what the word (of God) meant in terms of the life of the poor and the slaves of whom she was representative."[18] These Anawim were dependent upon God and the divine attributes they most admired were that God was mighty, holy, and merciful. ". . . for he who is mighty has done great things for me, and holy is his name. And his mercy is on those who fear him . . ." (Luke 1:49-50).

> True, in none of her apparitions has Mary come out in favor
> of a living wage or aid to underdeveloped countries. But is it
> not significant that she has appeared only to the poor? Ber-
> nadette, the three children at Fatima, the two at La Salette,
> the five at Beauraing—all were either very poor or mem-
> bers of the working class. And to Mariette at Banneux,
> Mary announced, "I am the Virgin of the Poor."[19]

The Old Testament prophets warned that only a remnant would be saved (Amos 3:12, 5:15, 9:8-12; Isaiah 4:2-3, 6:13, 10:19-20, etc.). And this remnant would be among the poor and lowly (Zephaniah 2:3, 3:11-13). I Maccabees 1:11-15 tells how the rich and powerful forsook the faith for worldly gain. In contrast to them, Luke saw that salvation had come to the poor.

The Magnificat "was a hymn celebrating God's redemption of 'the lowly' and 'the poor,' composed in the early Jewish-Christian Church and later applied to Mary by the insertion" about God having regard for the low estate of his handmaiden who will henceforth "be called blessed by all generations."[20] Thus, Mary personifies the "lowly" in Israel, to whom salvation had come.

The phrase, "He has shown might with his arm" (Luke 1:51), recalls how God had once before led an oppressed people out of slavery—led them out "with a mighty hand and an outstretched arm" (Deuteronomy 6:21, 26:8 and *passim*). The canticle's final thoughts move back to the beginning of Israel's history: God "has upheld Israel his servant, ever mindful of his mercy; even as he promised our fathers, promised

Abraham and his descendants forever" (Luke 1:54-55). Just as Abraham "had received the promises at the beginning on behalf of the entire nation, so one woman Mary, received the fulfillment of those promises on behalf of the nation at the end of time."[21]

Contemporary Reflections on Justice

We have seen God's concern for the poor and the lowly in the Old Testament. We have seen Mary's testimony about it in the Magnificat. Can a 20th-century Magnificat be composed from a mosaic of breakthroughs on the part of Christians sensitive to justice? We surely hope so, because our world is so pock-marked by unjust imbalances.

Consider, for example, just two imbalances, those with regard to energy consumption and to per capita income.

The United States (6% of the world's population) consumes five or six times its share of the world's energy. "This includes, in the mid-1970s, 33 percent of the annual world consumption of oil, 63 percent of natural gas, and 22 percent of coal."[22] Our per capita energy use is double that of West Germany, Sweden, France—countries with comparable living standards. Our per capita energy use is three or four times that of Japan and 340 times that of Ethiopia.

Less than 30 percent of the people control and consume more than 70 percent of the world's resources.

> Furthermore, the gap between rich and poor is growing wider. Item: in 1960, 25 tons of rubber (the sort of resource produced by a poor country) could buy 6 tractors (the sort of product sold by a rich country). In 1976, 25 tons of rubber bought 2 tractors. Item: According to World Bank President Robert McNamara the developing world's per capita income, adjusted for inflation, will increase $3 for the period 1970-1980 (from $105 to $108) while that of the developed world will increase $900 (from $3,100 to $4,000). For one fourth of the earth's 4 billion people income for the decade 1965-1975 grew at an annual rate of only 1.5% or $2 a year.[23]

In the face of such imbalances, consider the example of some astute people whose hearts bear Magnificat sentiments.

One such group has been the Capuchins. Before the 1979 revolution, 31 Capuchins protested to President Anastasio Somoza because of the violation of the human rights of people working for a better distribution and control of the land in Nicaragua. Within a year or two, Michael Crosby, OFM, another Capuchin, learned that Bankers Trust of New York had lent Somoza a great deal of money. The Midwest Capuchin Province had 500 shares in Bankers Trust. As Crosby wrote, "While the province was ministering and praying for justice on the level of the individual and group, it was unwittingly investing monies to reinforce the . . . infrastructure which systematically countered our part in the efforts to bring justice and peace to Nicaragua!"[24] Filing a shareholder resolution, the Capuchins persuaded Bankers Trust not to make additional loans to Somoza's Nicaragua. No more were Capuchins to benefit from extending this structure of oppression, while praying and ministering to overcome this same oppression.

Many other groups today participate in justice/peace efforts to ride herd on investment portfolios in order to insure the latter's more positive impact on the world. Seventeen Protestant denominations and 170 Catholic orders and dioceses, through the Interfaith Center on Corporate Responsibility, presented nearly 500 shareholder resolutions to more than 100 companies between 1970 and 1980.[25] These resolutions were aimed at correcting social injury. This combined investment portfolio of more than $6 billion was used to pressure for more responsible corporate behavior.

Without consistency between what one's *private* right hand and what one's *social* left hand is doing, there is moral confusion. Christianity's valuing personal being, encouraging practical micro-charity (i.e., one-on-one charity), and urging self-sacrificial love can mask structural inequalities and social injustices. Moral confusion results when we participate in unethical and privileged socioeconomic structures while cultivating individual, practical, neighborly love. Our individual or personal benevolence is hypocritical if attended by blindness or unjust social relations. Macro-charity, or social love, is required. While the Christian combination of individual charity and social privilege has been morally cynical, Brian Hebblethwaite reminded us that Marxists have an opposite tendency toward moral cynicism:

If Christians have often shown a combination of high

individual moral idealism with social blindness, Marxists have equally often shown a combination of egalitarian social idealism with individual moral cynicism. Christianity is certainly open to moral criticism for its tendency towards connivance in social injustice. But Marxism is certainly open to moral criticism for its much more overt and deliberate neglect of individual rights and values. Its willingness to embrace any and every means to the achievement of its egalitarian ends, its tendency to neglect the problems of safeguards against the abuse of power by those who actually hold the power in the name of the people, and indeed its very subordination of individual ethics to social ethics (and sometimes its refusal to acknowledge even the moral nature of its own social idealism)—all this is open to trenchant moral criticism.[26]

Thus, analysis of what happens to both individual and social rights is required before we can have a holistic justice and before we can know which political economies to endorse as closely approximating God's justice in scripture. If our religious faith leads us to agree with Israelite piety that one's excess of power, riches, and prestige is to be used for the needy, then one contemporary way of doing that is through the ministry of corporate responsibility—using one's stocks to bring justice to the activities of corporations. Structures can be evangelized through the just shareholder resolutions of those who believe in a social gospel.

One recent use of the ministry of corporate responsibility for a peace and justice issue occurred March 31, 1983. Representatives of the Sisters of Charity, BVM, and twelve other Roman Catholic congregations of sisters and religious brothers in the Chicago area held a Holy Week anti-nuclear weapons service on the University of Chicago's campus at the Henry Moore sculpture that commemorates the first sustained nuclear reaction. These congregations announced withdrawal of a combined $1.8 million invested in stock and bonds of fifteen major nuclear weapons contractors, including AT&T, Boeing, DuPont, Westinghouse, Tenneco, GE, ETE, and IBM. As the *BVM Center News* (June 1983) explained, "Listening to the Vatican describe 'over-production of military devices and the extent of unsatisfied vital needs, is in itself an act of aggression' (Declaration of Disarmament, 1976), the BVM congregation divested itself of stock in companies involved in the production, research and development of nuclear weapons."[27]

As loudly implied earlier in this paper, biblical sensitivity to justice should flow into any legal order formed by societies influenced by the Jewish-Christian ethic. However, this sensitivity soon leads one to an increasingly complex issue involved in justice matters—namely, that rights have often been violated in the history of the distribution of holdings (property, wealth). Would that we could confidently assume that the rights of minorities, the weak, and the poor have been assiduously protected throughout the whole historical process.

Joseph Holland of the Center for Concern in Washington, D.C., analyzed three structural stages of world industrialization: the 19th century laissez-faire state, the social welfare state or Progressive era from 1900 to 1968, and the national security state from 1968 onward. Because of international competition, national economies move toward state coordination. Because of security problems from competing states and marginalized social classes, police, military, and intelligence agencies loom larger administratively. The state becomes a larger consumer of armaments, and government social services are cut. Economically, there is "advanced capital-intensive technology and a maturing transnational market system,"[28] with deep unemployment. Culturally, freedom is redefined as security for a few while most are insecure.

To create a new global civilization, we must continue experiments aimed at humanizing the structures that cause destructive competition and that marginate people and erode democracy. Holland hinted at economic experiments to regulate the world market system to serve human needs. He challenged us to figure out a way to decentralize and yet have local community control over the formation of capital and social investment. Perhaps the most important creativity will be required culturally in order to read the signs of the times—to come up with new visions and new values. Will we not have to rethink "the relation of the individual and group, of humanity and nature, of production and reproduction, and of truth and mystery"?[29] The Center of Concern draws our attention to four key creators and carriers of a worthwhile vision: (1) the poor; (2) women; (3) labor movements reaching out in solidarity among skilled and unskilled, employed and unemployed, rural and urban laborers; and (4) world religions inspiring the humanization of structures.

Since wages distribute the capital produced by society, organizing for just wages is an important activity of justice-makers. Various other measures also help correct the imbalances that build up between the haves and the have-nots. Capitalism may be made more morally tolerable by progressive taxation and by nationalization of certain key industries or services. In *Quadragesimo Anno* in 1931, Pope Pius XI said, ". . . certain kinds of property, it is rightly contended, ought to be reserved to the State since they carry with them a dominating power so great that [they] cannot without danger to the general welfare be entrusted to private individuals."[30] Also hearkening back to I John 3:17, Ambrose, Aquinas, etc., Paul VI recognized that "the right to private property is not absolute and unconditional. No one may appropriate surplus goods solely for his own private use when others lack the bare necessities of life."[31] Yet, protection of some private property helps protect against total control by the state. Our aim must be to work against the economic inequality and state control that destroy fellowship and equal dignity.

Contrary to the Communist economies of the East and the economic policies of Western socialist parties, John Paul II's *Laborem Exercens* emphasized workers' co-determination, and not just governmentally planned economies. But still the encyclical also stressed the planned economy[32] because leaving production and distribution to the free market favors the rich and powerful. And when production and distribution are left to the transnationals, their economic plan tends to maximize their profits instead of the well-being of all.

Therefore, the way to a just society today, according to this labor encyclical, is to combine a planned economy with worker democracy. Catholic social teaching in the past has been wary of socialism because a government powerful enough to control the economy might threaten local units that protected freedom. However, John XXIII complemented Pius XI's principle of subsidiarity by the principle of socialization (that higher levels of government must protect people when lower levels of authority cannot provide for the people). And, since about 1972, papal teaching recognizes the threat in Western society from the transnational corporations.[33]

Preferential affirmative action is another justice-creating measure for the groups who have not previously been affirmed for educational and employment opportunities in the United States, particularly blacks, Hispanics, Native Americans, and women.[34] Worldwide, the feminization of poverty is seen starkly in Gloria Steinem's observation that women do 67 percent of the work, receive 10 percent of the salaries, and own 1 percent of the property.[35]

In this situation in which we are trying to create a new global and humane civilization, we can surely continue to be inspired by the biblical understanding of justice hammered out 2,000 years ago in that small sandy country fought over by such large powers as Egypt, Assyria, Babylon, Greece, and Rome. No wonder its insights into justice today resonate, with Third World countries scrambled over by the East and West as spheres of influence. As poor nations become pawns in the struggles of the industrialized superpowers, Bishop Kalilombe reminds us of the African proverb: " 'When the elephants fight, it is the grass that suffers.' "[36]

It is but a short trek back and forth between these reflections on justice and reflections on Mary, the Mirror of Justice. This is because an important image of Mary that has re-emerged in our day is the image in which she is associated with the poor, the oppressed, the "anawim," most of whom are women. She symbolizes their liberation. Her solidarity with them, as her embrace of Elizabeth, expresses a sisterhood, a cohumanity, to which the whole church is invited. In such a supportive community, we move from competitive isolation to the strength to do the works of justice.

As a symbol of faith, Mary helps transform political experience. It is not surprising, therefore, to find her appearance in the popular piety of Nicaraguans as they overthrew 46 years of dictatorship from the Somoza family. In the Novena of the Purisima—the feast of the Immaculate Conception—this Mirror of Justice was, in 1980, "hailed as one who helped the people defeat the Somocistas."[37] If we are to exalt the lowly and to fill the hungry with good things, we too may continue to need Magnificat Mary's inspiration.

We too can experience Mary's proof that "perceiving a new perceiving point, renews."[38] For Mary surely grasped that justice *is* the foundation of life, the cornerstone of human togetherness. She stands in the middle of a history that includes a Nathan bringing a justice-critique against the monarch David, a Jeremiah reproving rulers (Jeremiah 22:13f), an Isaiah and Amos reprimanding priests, and a Theresa Kane (a woman of mercy) trying to get through to a pope. While honoring Mary as "mother of justice and of social love," and seeing that through human work, "justice and social love are formed, if the whole working sector is governed by a just moral order,"[39] John Paul II and many other churchmen have not yet grown in the appreciation that there should be no discrimination even in the liturgy—the work of the people. Nor should women continue to be excluded from the positions in which the church's official decisions are made. Mary and all justice-seekers know that if the roots of hunger, poverty, and oppression are to be tackled, social love encourages us critically to examine the power relationships in *all* our systems, from "church" systems prohibiting altar girls to "defense" systems constructing first-strike nuclear weapons. May Mary motivate the church to tap the gifts of all as this fledgling church responds more deeply to involvement in systemic and perspectival change.

88 Mary According to Women

Footnotes

1 Richard P. McBrien, *Catholicism, Volume Two* (Minneapolis: Winston, 1980) p. 896

2 Richard P. McBrien, "Dogma," *Chicago Studies,* 20/2 (Summer, 1981), p. 149 Charles Curran explains that mediation is "the basic characteristic of the Catholic theological tradition. The Catholic tradition has recognized the importance of *and*: scripture and tradition; faith and reason; Jesus and the church." (*Moral Theology: A Continuing Journey.* Notre Dame: University of Notre Dame Press, 1982, pp. 219-220)

3 Synod of Bishops, *Justice in the World* (Washington, D.C.: United States Catholic Conference, 1972), p. 34

4 José Miranda, *Marx and the Bible: A Critique of the Philosophy of Oppression* (Maryknoll: Orbis, 1974), p. 93

5 Stephen Mott, "Egalitarian Aspects of the Biblical Theory of Justice," *Selected Papers from the Nineteenth Annual Meeting of the American Society of Christian Ethics* (1978), pp. 13-14

6 Foster R. McCurley and John H. Reumann, "Righteousness/Justice in Matthew," in George W. Forell and William H. Lazareth (eds.), *God's Call to Public Responsibility* (Philadelphia: Fortress, 1978), p. 32

7 U.S. Catholic Bishops, "Statement on Central America," *Maryknoll* (July, 1982), p. 1

8 John R. Donahue, S.J., "Biblical Perspectives on Justice," in John C. Haughey, S.J. (ed.), *The Faith That Does Justice: Examing the Christian Sources for Social Change* (New York: Paulist, 1977), p. 78

9 *Ibid.,* pp. 84-85

10 Marina Warner, *Alone of All Her Sex: the Myth and the Cult of The Virgin Mary* (New York: Alfred A. Knopf, 1976), p. 12

11 Raymond Brown, *The Birth of the Messiah* (Garden City: Doubleday, 1977), p. 360

12 *Ibid*

13 Arturo Paoli, *Meditations on Saint Luke* (Maryknoll: Orbis, 1972), p. 186

14 *Ibid.,* p. 196

15 *Ibid.,* p. 198

16 Raymond E. Brown, "Mary in the New Testament and in Catholic Life," *America* (May 15, 1982), p. 376

17 Mary Gordon, "Coming to Terms With Mary," *Commonweal* (January 15, 1982), p. 13

18 Brown, "Mary in the New Testament and in Catholic Life," *op. cit.,* p. 379

19 William Behringer, *Mary and the Beatitudes* (Staten Island: Alba House, 1964), p. 80

20 John McHugh, *The Mother of Jesus in the New Testament* (Garden City: Doubleday, 1975), p. 73

21 *Ibid.,* p. 79

22 Bruce C. Birch and Larry L. Rasmussen, *The Predicament of the Prosperous* (Philadelphia: Westminster, 1978), p. 34. For data supporting the argument that most environmental deterioration in the U.S. since 1940 results from growing affluence and changed consumption patterns, see Arthur J. Dyck's *On Human Care* (Nashville: Abingdon, 1977), p. 41

23 *Ibid.,* p. 38. Using far more resources, the first world is able to produce more gross national product (GNP) per capita, that is, more goods and services per person per

year. The first world (U.S., W. Europe, Japan) produces $5,000 or more in the amount of goods and services per person; the second world (USSR, E. Europe) produces between $2,000 and $5,000 worth of goods and services per person; the third world (Latin America, Africa, Asia) produces less than $2,000 worth of goods and services per person. [Barbara Cerny, BVM, and Eloise Thomas, BVM, "Reflections on a Third World Experience," (Salt: Winter, 1981), p. 4]

24 Michael Crosby, O.F.M. Cap., *Spirituality of the Beatitudes* (Maryknoll: Orbis, 1981), p. 103

25 Oliver Williams and John Houck, (eds.), *The Judeo-Christian Vision and the Modern Corporation* (Notre Dame: University of Notre Dame Press, 1982), p. 75

26 Brian Hebblethwaite, *Christian Ethics in the Modern Age* (Philadelphia: Westminster, 1982), pp. 35-36

27 During this Maundy Thursday ceremony at the Henry Moore sculpture commemorating the birthplace of the atomic bomb, "Sister Mary Frances Schafer, BVM, said the date and place were chosen because Holy Thursday is the day of transition from the sorrow and death themes of Lent to the peace and justice of Easter," *Chicago Sun Times* (April 2, 1983), p. 11. Also cf. *Chicago Sun Times* (April 1, 1983), p. 14, and *Chicago Tribune* (April 1, 1983), section 2, p. 3

28 Joseph Holland, "People and Jobs in the New International Economic Order: Humanizing the Third Stage of Industrialization," in *Convergence Proceedings, op. cit.*, p. 15. Also cf. Joe Holland and Peter Henriot, S.J., *Social Analysis: Linking Faith and Justice* (Washington, D.C.: Center of Concern, 1980) and cf. Joe Holland's review of Michael Novak's *The Spirit of Democratic Capitalism* in the *National Catholic Reporter* (May 7, 1982), pp. 12-13

29 *Ibid.*, p. 16

30 Par. 114 of "Quadragesimo Anno Encyclical of Pope Pius XI on Reconstruction of the Social Order, May 15, 1931," in Claudia Carlen, IHM, *The Papal Encyclicals*, Volume 3, a Consortium Book (Wilmington, North Carolina: McGrath Publishing Company, 1981), p. 433

31 Par. 23 of "Populorum Progressio Encyclical of Pope Paul VI on the Development of People, March 26, 1967," in Claudia Carlen, IHM, *op. cit.*, Volume 5, p. 187. In Charles E. Curran's judgment, "the very first thing that a Christian must say about worldly goods is that the goods of creation exist to serve the needs of all. This is the understanding found in recent documents of the World Council of Churches and of conciliar and papal Catholic social teaching. Pope Paul VI in his encyclical *Populorum Progressio* [par. 22] asserted, 'All other rights whatsoever, including those of property and of free commerce, are to be subordinated to this principle.'" Charles E. Curran's *Moral Theology: A Continuing Journey* (Notre Dame: University of Notre Dame Press, 1982), pp. 223-224

32 Section 18 (paragraphs 82-87) of "Laborem Exercens Encyclical of Pope John Paul II on Human Work, September 14, 1981," in Claudia Carlen, IHM, *ibid.*

33 Gregory Baum, *The Priority of Labor: A Commentary on Laborem Exercens, Encyclical Letter of Pope John Paul II* (New York: Paulist, 1982)

34 Daniel C. Maguire, *A New American Justice: Ending the White Male Monopolies* (Garden City, New York: Doubleday & Company, 1980)

35 Gloria Steinem's address in Des Moines, Iowa (cf. *The Des Moines Register*, April 20, 1983, p. 3M). Such imbalances can be critiqued on the basis of Vatican II's document on "The Church Today," section 29: "For excessive economic and social differences between the members of the one human family or population groups cause

scandal, and militate against social justice, equity, the dignity of the human person, as well as social and international peace," Walter Abbott (ed.), *The Documents of Vatican II* (New York: Guild Press, 1966), p. 228. Also see section 69 of the same document. Nor is there economic equality in the United States where women earn 59¢ for every dollar earned in wages by men. And the National Organization for Women has calculated that "over a lifetime, a woman who has auto, health, disability, and life insurance, and an annuity, will pay $16,732 *more* than a man will pay for the *same* coverage" (letter from Judy Goldsmith, president of NOW, July, 1983)

36   Most Rev. Patrick Kalilombe, WF, "Center and Periphery," in *Convergence Proceedings, op. cit.,* p. 20

37   Sheila D. Collins, "Feminist Theology at the Crossroads," *Christianity and Crisis* (December 14, 1981), p. 344

38   From "Our Lady, for Marilyn Hacker," in *Admit Impediment, Poems by Marie Ponsot* (New York: Alfred A. Knopf, 1981)

39   Pope John Paul II, "The Right of Polish Workers to Dialogue," *Origins* (July 7, 1983, p. 147

MARY OF NAZARETH
PARADIGM OF A PEACEMAKER
Mary Lauranne Lifka, BVM

Secular and sacred literature abounds in descriptions of peace. They range from public negative statements, such as the absence of war, to private positive descriptions, such as inner calm. The *Oxford English Dictionary* alone lists more than a dozen definitions. The Hebrew scriptures contain the word for peace more than 220 times. Nuances denote temporal prosperity as well as religious blessing. Indeed, few concepts are clear enough in themselves to be unqualified by the company they keep.

Words carry what their users think about the phenomena they signify. These words, in turn, provide glimpses into basic convictions of the people themselves about their lives and the world in which they live. Hence it is particularly instructive to look at the words for peace in three cultures that have affected our American society, for the three words show significant differences in what people understand peace to mean.

We start with the Hebrew meaning, since it is central to our sacred tradition. The semitic word for peace, *šalòm,* basically means "completeness" or "wholeness." Related to the noun form is the verbal root, *šlm* or *shalem.* In its various forms it can mean "to be complete," "to make whole," "to finish," and "to make an end of." Thus, the Hebrews meant a condition of human society in which there are completeness, unity, fullness—all thoroughly affirmative words. In its fullest sense, "shalom" is a religious term.

It refers to a gift of God (Isaiah 45:7), who makes people conscious of order and thereby liberates them from chaos, vindicates the righteous, punishes the guilty, and estab-

lishes justice for the oppressed. . . . [Peace] is freely
given to Israel as a gift from God as long as Israel chooses
the way of obedience.[1]

The words for peace in Greek and Latin have negative connotations.
"Peace is seen as the absence or suspension of strife."[2] This understanding has influenced our secular tradition.

The Greek word, *eirene,* "does not primarily denote a relationship
between several people . . . but a state of affairs . . . conceived of
. . . as an interlude in the everlasting state of war."[3] Originally a political term, *eirene* also stands for a truce. Our English words "irenic" and
"irenical" mean "to promote peace, to be conciliatory or pacific."

The Latin word, *pax,* refers to an agreement or compact "established
in the course of the unremitting struggle between conflicting interests."[4]
Romans looked upon peace not as a normal part of the human condition but as an unusual temporary state of affairs.

These three different understandings of peace suggest the following
general statement: how a group of people defines peace affects their
culture's attitudes about the value and pursuit of peace. We find evidence for this generalization in the Bible.

Scripture contains a detailed theory of peace. Its first point is an
eschatological focus. Isaiah prophesied that "in the days to come"
people will live together in peace.

> They shall beat their swords into plowshares
> and their spears into pruning hooks;
> One nation shall not raise the sword against another,
> nor shall they train for war again (Isaiah 2:2-4).[5]

Full-scale peace will coincide with the coming of the messianic kingdom
of the "Prince of Peace" (Isaiah 9:6). This future thrust elicits our belief
and action.

The second trait of the biblical theory of peace appears at the dawn of
society. Genesis teaches that peace holds a primordial place in human
existence, for peace was the original condition of man and woman.
Their nature, essentially peaceable, fulfills itself in peace. Conversely,
war is not their normal condition, but a corruption of their condition.
"It must always be remembered," John Macquarrie, Oxford don, has
alerted us, "that in biblical teaching righteousness is more original than
sin."[6] This historical sequence needs to be established because our

Western theological emphasis on sin, on original sin, has periodically distorted the correct chronology.

Speculation about the impact of (1) the negative connotations of peace voiced in classical tongues, (2) a theme of human sinfulness in patristic literature, and (3) the warlike aggressive behavior in kingdoms and nations helps us to see unfavorable conditions for peace in the world. Despite inimical trends, the Bible affirms righteousness to be more fundamental than sin. The Bible proclaims God's gift of peace in the covenant theme and the marital fidelity metaphor. Therefore, in principle, peace is more integral to our lives than is war.

The third attribute of the biblical theory of peace is its synergism in a given age. This dynamism in a specific time flows from the dialectic of the other two characteristics; namely, eschatological or future time and primordial or past time. Peace is not simply a static condition of being. Rather, peace is "a process and a task as [persons] move from potentiality to realization."[7]

For the prophets, peace graced temporal conditions. For example, Hosea (5:8-14, 14:2-10) saw peace in the thick of political troubles as the threat of Assyria against Israel loomed large. Zechariah felt that "now . . . is the seed-time of peace: the vine shall yield its fruit, the land shall bear its crops, and the heavens shall give their dew" (8:12). Micah complained of fair-weather sages "who, when their teeth have something to bite, announce peace, but when one fails to put something in their mouth, proclaim war against him" (3:5).

The temporal dynamism of biblical peace also marked the Hebrews' quest toward truth and justice. Jeremiah cried, "They would repair, as though it were nought, the injury to my people. 'Peace, peace!' they say, though there is no peace" (6:14).[8] The psalmist pleaded for divine aid against a powerful league of hostile nations (Psalm 83).[9] The thirteen historical books narrate the Israelites' efforts to establish, in a word, peace, among themselves, with their neighbors, and before Yahweh.

The Old Testament theory of peace with its three-phase time-frame of future, past, and present proved central to Jesus' thought. Reared in the Jewish faith among Palestinians, he learned the Aramaic and Hebrew meanings of shalom. So much did he value peace that he gave it to his disciples as though it were a legacy. "Peace I leave with you, my peace I give to you" (John 14:27, Macquarrie translation). Thus, in one rich concept, he conveyed his intent and his mission. When instructing his missioners, he referred to peace as a force or a charge they could give to others. "As you enter the house, bless it. If the house is deserving, your peace will descend on it. If not, your peace [or blessing] will return to you" (Matthew 10:11-12, Wansbrough translation).[10]

Jesus' life and work shaped the New Testament writers' statements about peace. Paul expressed its importance in one sentence: "It is he who is our peace, and who made the two of us one by breaking down the barrier of hostility that kept us apart" (Ephesians 2:14). Luke described the flourishing condition of the early Christians "throughout all Judea, Galilee, and Samaria" as peace (Acts 9:31).

In using peace to bond Jesus with Christians, the New Testament writers sought to ameliorate individuals' depth of alienation, society's resistance to peace, and the divisive hostilities and prejudices that plague people.

Matthew particularly wrote of dissension and the need for reconciliation. His chapter 18 dealt mainly with peaceful relations between neighbors. He exhorted the people to childlike openness and to concern rather than contempt for those who stray. He instructed the people on how to correct the errant. He assured them of Jesus' presence among the reconciled and promised them unlimited forgiveness. In this context, peace is not merely the absence of strife, or just a casual greeting of "Shalom," "Hi!" Rather, in Matthew's Judeo-Christian community, as in ours, peace required conscious efforts to overcome obstacles. Peace becomes a positive achievement. No wonder Matthew counted the peacemakers among the eight groups who merit a beatitude (Matthew 5:9); the only blessing awarded for doing something, since the others reward attitudes.

Matthew's neighbors were not the only group to be instructed in the pride of peace. The Corinthians received a similar lesson.

In the port town of Corinth, dockworker, athlete, and hetaera rubbed shoulders. Paul found contention and disturbance among them. Whether it was pretension to wisdom, disregard of dietary rules, separate groupings at the eucharist, or gifts of the Spirit, disharmony rankled the community. Paul told the Corinthians—and us—that the only criterion for action is building peace in the society.[11]

First-generation Christians lived when peace coexisted with conflict.[12] Present-day believers are alerted more to large-scale crises than to calm.

The modern conquest of time and space, with the reduction of the earth to a global village, has drastically affected our ideas of peace and stress. Conditions today are such that authentic community can only mean worldwide fraternity and sorority. Americans, for example, can "be in" Beirut, Belfast, San Salvador, or Washington, D.C., courtesy of technology. Electronics can show us the planet on a fluorescent screen. Media display pain and turmoil as routine fare. Hence, many people in our culture now assume that peace is to be thought of as "nonwar," utopian and futuristic.

The research of contemporary Americans into war and peace can help us find our culture's understanding of these topics. In approaching them, a peace researcher, whether a political scientist, an investigative reporter, or an historian, brings certain convictions and preferences. These influence her work and its conclusions. Some peace researchers, for example, contend that true peace remains impossible without liberation from oppression and injustice. Others maintain that real peace presupposes world government.[13] All assert that being informed is the minimum requirement for peace in our time. Jonathan Schell has described such knowledge as "the full emotional, intellectual, spiritual, and visceral understanding. . . . "[14]

In her work, the peace researcher, on the one hand, uses historical data and, on the other, imagination in building a paradigm or a framework of analysis. Berenice Carroll, professor of political science at the University of Illinois-Urbana, has described the process:

> Historical events are neither entirely unique nor fully determined by known laws. One may draw upon the past for guidance in the formulation of social policy, not with certainty but with a degree of confidence related to the depth and breadth of one's knowledge of pertinent experience of the past.

She has argued that:

> If we are "to make sense" of the great diversity of historical experience it must be, ultimately, through analyzing its complexities, collating, classifying and generalizing.[15]

In an effort to make sense of that diverse historical experience, let us consider four explanations of uneven worth about how societies seek to build peaceful communities.[16]

One hypothesis suggests that peace within a nation is achieved through projection. This model juxtaposes war and peace by postulating that societies that are conflict-ridden use external aggression in order to get internal cohesion. Attempts to validate the projection hypothesis have not yielded high correlations between domestic agitation and foreign aggression. Historical evidence, however, suggests that democratic societies are less consciously belligerent, while developed societies are more deliberately belligerent. So far no one has calibrated the belligerence of a society at once democratic and developed like the U.S.A.

A second explanation is based on the popular notion that a rise in the standard of living or a fairer distribution of the fruits of labor would contribute significantly to a more peaceful world. Studies discredit this idea. In fact, research indicates that, while a more equitable distribution may ease a society's internal problems, it frees resources for external aggression at the same time.[17]

The third and fourth explanations are models peace researchers use to account for systems of international peace. Both are based on power, that ability to obtain compliance and to affect the course of events.

The first model is that of minimum equality among members. The explanation rests on the premise that an international system can be best served by making power the monopoly of one nation or bloc of nations. Historical examples for this pattern include the Pax Romana of the ancient period, the Pax Ecclesia of the Middle Ages, and the Pax Britannica of the modern era. Current efforts to wield power in the mode of minimal equality are the Pax Americana and the Pax Sovietica.

The second model for an international peace system is that of maximum equality among members. In the nineteenth century, this pattern formed the "balance of power" because no nation or alliance had the strength to supplant or defeat another. In contemporary times, this pattern creates the "balance of terror" whereby war supposedly becomes impossible under the threat of mutual annihilation. In the Pax Atomica, the risk of annihilation is too great.[18]

The two models for international peace systems based on power, the notion that a fair distribution of goods brings peace, and the hypothesis of projection as a way to peace all point to the diverse paradigms or constructs of peace in secular literature. In this respect, peace resembles health,[19] a phenomenon difficult to grasp in its totality but sensed in its defects. Thus statements tend to be shaped by the perceptions of peace —or health—one has.

We are reminded that concepts are known in part by the company they keep. Small wonder that Johan Galtung of the University of Oslo has recommended that a peace plan "be classified not only according to its content but also according to who put it forward."[20] The advocates of a peace plan may be an individual or an organization. Either agent may be in (1) the decision-making center of a world system, (2) in the power center of a nation, or (3) on the periphery of a society. Working from the center or the periphery, the advocates of a peace plan face complexity.

Take the case of proponents of a peace plan who act apart from policymakers and hence are classified technically as a minority or at the margin of society. Peace researchers have observed that such advocates show

> an absolutist and moralistic, as opposed to a gradualist and pragmatic approach; a tendency toward single-factor, as opposed to multiple-factor thinking; and a tendency to confuse organizational levels, so that the training and capacity of the plan's author are made to seem more important than the possible merits of the plan itself.[21]

Peacemakers whose efforts are marked in this way include some sociologists who chart conflict-inducing social structures, some psychologists who concentrate on stressors, and some educators who command order and harmony in the schools. Historically such simplistic views have become the nuclei around which people of like minds have rallied for short-lived efforts.

Now, move to the case of a peace plan from decision-makers. Peace researchers have found that their proposals are likely to show signs of a gradualist pragmatic approach and multiple-factor thought. Careful not to tangle organizational procedures, authorities can act so slowly and so withdrawn from the public eye that tension between the power core and the society at large mounts. Impatience and confrontation then can

lead to demonstrations, factions, and other forms of protest. Historically, the results of peace plans from both groups have been mixed.

This brief survey indicates that the work of peace researchers has
been varied but instructive. It enables us to recognize the complexities
in peace. It challenges us to act upon the knowledge brought to our
attention, for peace research is but a means to a larger end; namely,
substantive success in individual efforts and group movements toward
peace.

Secular views of peace, however, do not complete our search for the
essence of peace. We now need to check the religious vision of the
Catholic Church.

The religious vision of peace has been framed most recently in the
"Pastoral Constitution on the Church in the Modern World (*Gaudium
et Spes*)," promulgated by the Second Vatican Council on December 7,
1965, and in the pastoral letter on "The Challenge of Peace," approved
by the American Catholic Bishops on May 3, 1983. Both documents
acknowledge that we in the nuclear age live in peril. The universal
pastoral has described "the whole human family fac[ing] an hour of
crisis." The national pastoral has described "the world . . . at a
moment of supreme crisis." Churchmen at the council traced peace to
the "harmony built into the human society by its divine Founder, and
actualized by men [sic] as they thirst after ever greater justice. . . ."[22]
The U.S. bishops defined peace as "both a divine gift and a human
work." They affirmed that

> the building of peace within and among nations is the work
> of many individuals and institutions; it is the fruit of ideas
> and decisions taken in the political, economic, social, mili-
> tary and legal sectors of life.

They asserted that "the church, as a community of faith and a social
institution, has a proper, necessary and distinctive part to play in the
pursuit of peace in the world."[23]

Speaking to the faithful at St. Mary of Czestochowa Church, Joseph
Cardinal Bernardin proclaimed that

> [the] call to peacemaking speaks with equal force to mem-
> bers of families who are quarreling and fighting, to mem-
> bers of different neighborhoods and communities who are
> in conflict, to ethnic and social groups which are at odds, to

governments of the world which amass nuclear armaments
and prepare for war.[24]

The call to make peace may be addressed to all sectors of society, but
church officials have ascribed a specific mission to women. In one of the
closing messages of the Second Vatican Council, the churchmen declared, "Women of the entire universe . . . you to whom life is entrusted at this grave moment in history, it is for you to save the peace of
the world."[25]

Women had not been allowed to speak in the council sessions, but
they had joined a peace lobby in going from bishop to bishop with a
draft of a peace statement. The text referred to the beatitudes as "not
only a way to personal perfection but also a power capable of transforming institutions and giving a new meaning to history."[26] These women
who had worked behind the scenes to persuade the churchmen to take a
stand on the war/peace issue were particularly moved by the plea in the
council's "Message to Women":

Reconcile men with life and above all, we entreat you,
watch carefully over the future of our race. Hold back the
hand of man who, in a moment of madness, might attempt
to destroy human civilization.[27]

In the light of these varied reflections on peace, we can come to an
operational definition: peace means an integrated and harmonious
functioning of an individual or a group. When rooted in truth and
watered with respect, such behavior yields well-being within a person
as well as within a community and among nations. With this description of peace in mind, we are prepared to look to Mary of Nazareth as a
peacemaker.

We need to recall that the New Testament speaks of Mary's active
presence more than her words. After the annunciation, we meet her
traveling to visit her pregnant cousin Elizabeth, to her husband Joseph's ancestral home, and to Egypt. Once settled back in Nazareth,
she searches for her lost boy, attends a wedding reception, listens to her
adult son preach. Then she stands at his execution on Calvary. The last
mention of her is waiting in the upper room. In all, her behavior foreshadowed to Jesus "the Christian way—making peace, tendering mercy,
calling fervently for justice."[28]

Mary's presence at the wedding in Cana has occasioned much commentary from patristic time to our times. American Catholic bishops used the Cana episode in their 1973 pastoral letter, "Behold Your Mother: Woman of Faith." Of her role at the wedding feast, they wrote, "We see her quick grasp of the situation, her willingness to make compassionate intercession."[29] Of her action there, Barbara Thomas, SCN, past president of the Leadership Conference of Women Religious, observed, "[W]e find her fearlessly taking the initiative . . . she urged her son to the first manifestation of his power at Cana."[30] Patricia Noone, SC, teacher of women's studies at the College of Mt. St. Vincent in Riverdale, N.Y., has noted that Mary "is shown as enabling Christ to take a dramatic step of self-exposure and decisively begin his public ministry."[31] Mary Frances Shafer, past president of the Sisters of Charity of the Blessed Virgin Mary, declared, "We are challenged by the words she spoke among friends at a wedding feast. 'Whatever he tells you to do—do it!' " Shafer concluded, "Through her intercession we have hope of receiving the gift of peace. By following her example we also have hope of sharing that gift of peace."[32]

Literary Form of the Fourth Gospel

To build our case for Mary as a paradigm of a peacemaker, we set the verses about the Cana wedding feast into the framework of John's composition.[33] He wrote his gospel on a liturgical plan. That is, in John's account of the good news, "it is around the occasion of the liturgical feasts of Israel that Jesus develops His mission, and it is on their symbolism that He builds His teaching."[34] Thus an outline of the gospel corresponds to the six liturgical feasts Jesus attended,[35] where he performed his signs[36] and presented his message.

Prologue. "The Word became flesh . . . we saw his glory" (1:1-18).

The Opening week of seven days finishing with the first sign at Cana:

The water changed into wine (1:19-2:12).

The First Passover and return to Galilee through Judea and Samaria,

finishing with the second sign at Cana:

The healing of the nobleman's son (2:13-4:54).
The Second Feast, perhaps Pentecost:
The sign of the healing of the sick woman at Bethesda.
The other Passover: the signs of the multiplying of the bread and the walking on the lake.
The Feast of Tabernacles, in the autumn:
The sign of the healing of the man born blind (7:1-10:21).
The Feast of the Dedication, in winter:
The sign of the resurrection of Lazarus (10:22-11:54).
The week of the Passion (11:55-18:27).
The Last Passover; the sign of the elevation on the Cross and the thrusting in of the spear, which gives birth to the Church (18:28-19:42).
The final week of the appearances of the Resurrection:
From the Sunday of the Passover to the Sunday of Thomas:
The signs of the Resurrection finishing with the words about faith in signs without the sight of signs:
"Blessed are those who believe and have not seen" (20:1-29).
Conclusion to the Gospel of the signs (20:30-31).
Appendix on the life of the Church and the return of Christ (21:1-23)
with a new ending alluding to signs (21:24-25; cf. 21:25 with 20:30).[37]

The mention of days, the literary parallelisms, and the details of events convey John's theological intent in proclaiming the life of Jesus. A case in point is his literary use of time, of precise days for the opening week of Jesus' ministry. It is at the end of this period that the sign at Cana occurred.

First Day: The first witness of John the Baptist:
"I am not the Christ . . . he is coming" (1:19-28).
Second Day: The second witness of John the Baptist:
"Behold the lamb of God who taketh away the sin of the world. . . .
"I have seen the Spirit like a dove descending from the

heavens resting on him. He is the chosen of God" (1:29-34).

Third Day: The calling of Andrew and another disciple of John the Baptist:
"Behold the lamb of God." "Come and see" (1:35-9):
The calling of Simon Peter (1:40-42).

Fourth Day: The calling of Philip:
"Follow me!" (1:43-44).
The calling of Nathanael:
"Rabbi, thou art the Son of God, the king of Israel" (1:45-51).

The Seventh Day: The marriage at Cana, the seventh day after the calling of Philip and Nathanael.[38]

The impossibility of commuting around Galilee in the manner implied by the rapid succession of events in John 1:19-51 indicates that the evangelist did not mean calendar time. Rather he meant mystical or symbolic time reminiscent of the priestly writer's use of time in the Genesis account of creation. For example, the Prologue of John's gospel begins like Genesis: "In the beginning . . . " (Genesis 1:1; John 1:1). Max Thurian, a Brother of Taizé, explained that "the Evangelist wishes to show that the messianic salvation is a new creation in Christ, the Word which was at the beginning by which all was made" (1:1-3) "and which has become flesh" (1:14).[39] In a symbolic week, John credits Jesus with the foundation of a new order, the messianic community of the church. Then, on the seventh day, the sign of rest, John has Jesus enjoy a village marriage celebration "which symbolizes and prefigures the eschatological marriage of God with his people, the messianic banquet of the Kingdom."[40]

This kind of use of a secular event to represent a sacred act distinguishes John's literary style. Rosemary Ruether observed that
John's gospel is built on the contrast between the fleshy level of reality, where all is blindness and disbelief, and the spiritual level of redeeming insight. Jews, Jesus' family, and even disciples are foils of the realm of darkness and unbelief against which the drama of revelation is played out.[41]

With respect to the wedding celebration, feminist theologian Ruether has noted that "Jesus' miracle at Cana is a sign that the old waters of purification, i.e. Jewish law, have been superseded by the 'new wine' of the gospel."[42] In similar fashion, John McHugh, professor of theology at Upshaw Seminary in Durham, England, has described the Cana episode as "purification water of Judaism."[43]

Specifically, the Johannine Cana text serves theological purposes, not documentary interests. This interpretation draws strength from pointing out three omissions that would have been included in a witness's account. Indeed, no mention is made of the bride and groom whose nuptials occasioned the party. No description of the thaumaturge's behavior adds drama. And no mention of the guests' reaction to the new wine confirms the headwaiter's comment to the groom. In a narrative so selective in details, the mention of Mary three times "can have no explanation other than a deliberate [Marian] doctrinal explanation."[44]

The Story of the Wedding at Cana

So that our paradigm with Mary as a peacemaker may be derived in a genuine manner from the Johannine text, we must analyze the three verses on which the thesis depends. These are:

v. 3 . . . the mother of Jesus told him,
"They have no wine."
v. 4 Jesus replied, "Woman, what is that to me and to thee? My hour is not yet come."
v. 5 His mother instructed those waiting on table,
"Do whatever he tells you."[45]

Our analysis involves why Mary intervened in a matter that, strictly speaking, was the responsibility of the host, the intended meaning of Jesus' words to Mary, and the real meaning of Mary's directive to the waiters.

We want to avoid the tortured and convoluted exegeses of the three enigmatic verses in the familiar English rendition. To do so we "tesser." That is, we jump the time barrier and go to the point of the evangelist's writing. We look for literary sources that may have been the basis for the gospel Cana narrative.

In reviewing the numerous attempts to find the source John may have adapted, McHugh noted, "perhaps the most remarkable feature of

these reconstructions is the degree to which they coincide." With the
caveat that "significant differences do occur between one author and the
next," he conceded that, in the end, individuals must make up their own
minds.[46]

Based on literary criteria, McHugh demonstrated that "If all charac-
teristically Johannine words, phrases and constructions are taken to be
insertions by the evangelist, and only those verses which do not contain
any typically Johannine usage retained, then a perfectly coherent story
emerges."[47] It reads:

1. There was a wedding in Cana of Galilee,
   and the mother of Jesus was there.

2. Now Jesus also had been invited,
   with his disciples, to the wedding.

3. So when wine ran short,
   the mother of Jesus told him,
   They have no wine.

6. Now there were six stone water-pots standing there,
   for the Jewish custom of purification,
   each having a capacity of two or three firkins.[48]

7. (So) Jesus said to (the waiters)
   Fill the water-pots with water;
   and they filled them right up to the top.

8. Then he said to them,
   Now draw some out and take it to the head waiter.
   So they took it.

9. And as soon as the head waiter had tasted the water,
   he called the bridegroom

10. and said to him,
    every man serves the good wine first,
    and when men are half-drunk, that which is inferior;
    but thou hast kept the good wine until now.

11. This Jesus did as the beginning of signs,
    in Cana of Galilee.[49]

Thereby the rendition stands free from the apparent *non sequitur* in
verses three through five.

This version tells a miracle story with a marked brevity or economy
of words. Its thrust is toward the impact of the marvel on the head

waiter. It resembles the miracle accounts found in the synoptic gospels. Let us accept the scholars' claim that the evangelist of the fourth gospel drew upon a traditional tale rather than wrote an original one. Let us assume that he had before him the terse but poignant story cited above.

This version contains no exchange between Jesus and Mary, no directive from her to the servers. Yet even this form of the Cana story would impress its listeners as a wonder, a miracle, an astounding event. But would it convey to its listeners that here was a sign or symbol of something veiled from natural human sight but visible to the eyes of faith? Probably not. McHugh reasoned that the evangelist "decided to make the sign value evident by inserting a short dialogue between Jesus and his mother."[50]

To gauge accurately the import of John's insertion of verses 4 and 5, we must pay attention to context and syntax, for the historian's basic rule is that an authentic document must be explicated so that it makes sense.

In verse 3, "the mother of Jesus told him, 'They have no wine.' " Use of the accusative case instead of the dative after the Greek verb "to say" is so unusual and emphatic that its use carries a deliberate message. The syntax of Mary's statement indicates that she is not merely remarking on an embarrassment. Rather she is directly suggesting that Jesus take action. The doctrinal explanation for Mary's intervention in a matter that strictly speaking was not her affair becomes clear. Mary's words are to initiate Jesus' sign.

John has Jesus reply, "Woman, what is that to me and to thee? My hour is not yet come."[51]

Admittedly, the majority of commentators from patristic ancients to learned moderns have interpreted this reply to mean Jesus is rebuking Mary.

Not so! Verse 4 bears the distinctive hallmarks of Johannine style. John's syntax indicates that both Jesus and Mary share a realization. They recognize the implications in the moment. They sense that the final hour, or his decisive act, approaches. But they face it with some trepidation. John's wording is equivalent to the Semitic expression *mah-li walak* found in the Old Testament in similar passages of reluctance. Users of this phrase feel confronted by hostility or an unpleasant situation.[52]

Perhaps we would better comprehend verse 4 were it translated differently: "Is this the time for me to get on with my father's business?" Or use the question that comes to mind when responsibility calls: "Do I have to do it now?"

We need to explore more fully the interpretation that verse 4 conveys a shared understanding between Jesus and Mary. On the surface, she has just asked for earthly wine to avert an awkward scene at a wedding celebration. Jesus then alerts her to the inner significance of his imminent action. Through Jesus' reply to Mary's observation, John directs his listeners to that action.[53]

At a deeper level, "the shortage of wine is both providential and intentional in order that the miracle can take place."[54] How appropriate to the biblical tradition describing Yahweh's relation to the Chosen People in terms of the marriage bond that it was wedding guests who first shared "the beginning of the signs" through which Jesus revealed his glory![55] The Johannine marriage story points to "a marvelous sign which manifests the glory of the Messiah and awakens the faith of the disciples."[56] Only after the account of the miracle, the result of Mary's initiative, do we learn that Jesus' "disciples believed in him."[57]

John's narrative portrays Mary as standing with Jesus opposite the others. In John's account of the Cana miracle, Jesus speaks to Mary as a believer already aware of Jesus' mission to provide not physical but spiritual nourishment. Thus he addressed her, not as mother by virtue of her blood ties, but as "woman" because of her faith.[58] How logical then for Mary to follow Jesus' words as she did. She instructs the waiters, "Do whatever he tells you."

McHugh saw in Mary's directive a model of the church in action. "The church which knows the nature of Jesus' mission" tells "the world which is hungry for material blessings" to do whatever Jesus says and we will be astonished at the result.[59]

Mary as Peacemaker

How does the Johannine account of Mary's role at the wedding contribute to a paradigm[60] of a peacemaker? To answer this question, we consider the Cana text in terms of peace and conflict and move through the passage on two levels: (a) its surface meaning or face value, and (b) its deeper significance or its exemplary value.

Suppose those who had accepted the wedding invitation felt insulted by their host's breach in hospitable customs. Trouble could flare. What if some revelers sparked a ruckus over the perceived injustice of inadequate food and drink? Would hostilities have divided the villagers into factions? What if some miffed guests let the apparent neglect of their welfare corrode ties to their neighbors? In any case, peace would be strained.

Mary of Nazareth appreciated peace. Reared in the Jewish tradition, familiar with Hebrew, and conversant in Aramaic, she would have understood that *shalem* means to make whole or make complete. She would have known that peace refers to a condition of society whereby its members share fullness or unity. Invited to the wedding celebration, she would naturally anticipate an enjoyable time. Like any guest, she would assume that the festive arrangements had been completed. She would expect unity, camaraderie, and even conviviality among the guests. Thus she would hope to share in the fullness of the occasion. Belonging to a culture that deeply valued hospitality, she would recognize imminent conflict when standard social conditions seemed awry. A sensitive, refined person, she reacted when the lack of wine augured ill for the celebrants.

Granted, in verse 1 of the Johannine Cana text, the identifying words, "the mother of Jesus," underscore Mary's unique physical relationship with the worker of signs. Yet she had her own part in the event. That part in the Cana episode is distinct from her role as the mother of Jesus. Already present at the outset of the celebration, she apparently came to the wedding feast on her own. Such independence is not unusual in view of the fact that ancient marriage festivities commonly lasted for seven days.[61]

Aware to some extent that her son "must be about [his] father's business," Mary turned to Jesus in her distress over the embarrassment caused when the wine ran out. She believed that harmony among the celebrants would be saved through his deed. Her "thirst after even greater justice," to use the words of *Gaudium et Spes,* led her to that "process and task" whereby "persons moved from potentiality to realization." Could she have sensed that her intervention was pivotal for the coming of the messianic kingdom of the Prince of Peace, foretold by Isaiah 9:5? Possibly.

Clearly, with her straightforward directive to the waiters, Mary showed full confidence in Jesus' power to "do whatever." With her directive to those responsible for provisions, she respected established routine and organizational structure. Like effective peacemakers in the secular arena and in the spiritual field, she did not impose her solution. Instead, she called forth the best in the participants in the crisis. That is, Jesus surrendered to his mission; the waiters obeyed his order.

Thus, on both the natural and supernatural levels, Mary is an agent of peace in the Cana crisis. She acts to bring about "the proper and harmonious functioning of a whole personality" and "the good relations between people."[62] Acting in truth, that is, in fidelity to the available facts, and with respect, that is, with regard for the individuality of those involved, she effected the well-being of her neighbors, as well as of future generations. Small wonder that subsequent believers called Mary queen of peace.[63]

Footnotes

1   Leslie Hoppe, "Bible Terms Today: *Shalom*—Peace," *The Bible Today*, p. 21 (May 1983), p. 202. John Macquarrie, *The Concept of Peace* (New York: Harper and Row, 1973), pp. 14-15. M. Rodriguez, "Peace (in the Bible)," *New Catholic Encyclopedia*, XI, p. 37

2   Macquarrie, *The Concept of Peace*, p. 15

3   *Ibid.* Quote from Werner Foerster, *Theological Dictionary of the New Testament*, G. Kittel (ed.), G.W. Bromiley II (trans.), p. 401

4   Macquarrie, *The Concept of Peace*, p. 15

5   All biblical citations are from the New American Bible translation, except as noted in the text. See Henry Wansbrough, "Blessed Are the Peacemakers," *The Way*, 22 (Jan. 1982), pp. 10-17

6   *The Concept of Peace*, p. 18

7   *Ibid.*, p. 19. Sexist "man" had been changed to "persons"

8   Also, "Justice will bring about peace; right will produce calm and security" (Isaiah 32:17). Rodriguez, "Peace (in the Bible)," p. 38. Wansbrough, "Blessed Are the Peacemakers," p. 12

9   From the Exodus to the monarchy, Hebrews looked to God as the warrior-leader. See Deuteronomy 1:30, 20:4; Joshua 2:24; Judges 3:28

10 Wansbrough, "Blessed Are the Peacemakers," p. 13. Michael Crosby, "Blessed Are the Peacemakers, for They Shall Be Called God's Children," *The Spirituality of the Beatitudes: Matthew's Challenge for First World Christians* (New York: Orbis, 1981), p. 179

11 Wansbrough, "Blessed Are the Peacemakers," p. 16

12 See St. Thomas 2a, 2ae, 29.2 and 4

13 Berenice Carroll, "Introduction: History and Peace Research," *Journal of Peace Research* 6 (Dec. 1969), p. 288

14 Jonathan Schell, "Reflections: The Fate of the Earth—Part III, The Choice," *The New Yorker*, Feb. 15, 1982, p. 98

15 Carroll, "Introduction: History and Peace Research," pp. 290-292. See also Clinton Fink, "Editorial Notes" and "Peace Research in Transition: A Symposium," *Journal of Conflict Resolution*, 16 (Dec. 1971), pp. 463-621

16 Johan Galtung, "Peace," *International Encyclopedia of the Social Sciences*, XI, p. 587. He has noted that interest in war leaves efforts for peace "speculative and value contaminated rather than analytical and empirical."

Concerning the contributions of the social sciences, see Charles Perrow, "Disintegrating Social Sciences," *Phi Delta Kappan*, 63 (June 1982), pp. 684-689. He has shown that the social sciences give the impression of rational behavior which masks the disorder and limitations of our everyday lives.

Admittedly, studies have focused more on wars as a unit than on peace. Like psychology which tells us more about mental illness than creativity, and news media which report more on riots and rebellion than on reconciliation and truces, political science recounts more about discord than tranquility in and among humans. We can, nonetheless, learn something about the meaning of large-scale peace from this literature.

17 Galtung, "Peace," p. 489

18 *Ibid.* For a cogent analysis of the illogic of the Pax Atomica, see Jonathan Schell,

"Reflections: The Fate of the Earth—Parts I, II and III," *The New Yorker,* Feb. 1, 8, and 15, 1982, pp. 47-114, 48-109, and 45-108

19   "Originally peace meant physical integrity," writes Mary Evelyn Jegen, SND, "Christian Spirituality, Disarmament and Security," *New Catholic World,* 225 (March, April 1982), p. 85

20   Galtung, "Peace," p. 494

21   *Ibid.,* p. 495. For examples of individual women at the margin, see Berenice Carroll, "The Outsiders: Comments on Eukuda Hideko, Catherine Marshall and Dorothy Detzer," *Peace and Change,* 4 (Fall 1977), pp. 23-26

22   *Gaudium et Spes,* section 78. *The Documents of Vatican II,* Walter Abbot (ed.) (New York: Guild Press, 1966), p. 290

23   Catholic Church, National Conference of Catholic Bishops, *The Challenge of Peace: God's Promise and Our Response* in *The Chicago Catholic,* April 8, 1983, p. 3-A

24   Joseph Bernardin, Homily for Aug. 28, 1982, reprinted in *The Chicago Catholic,* Installation Issue, Sept. 5, 1982, p. 83

25   Quoted in Eileen Egan, "Woman and the Peace Message of Jesus," *Catholic Worker,* 42 (Feb. 1976), p. 4

26   *Ibid.*

27   *Ibid.*

28   *Patricia Noone, Mary for Today* (Chicago: Thomas More Press, 1977), pp. 78-79. On biography, see James Reese, "This Historical Image of Mary in the New Testament," *Marian Studies* (Dayton: Mariological Society of America, 1977), pp. 27-44

29   Catholic Church, National Conference of Catholic Bishops, *Behold Your Mother: Woman of Faith* (Washington, D.C.: U.S. Catholic Conference, 1973), par. 36, p. 13

30   James Breig, "Mary, Mary Quite Contemporary," *U.S. Catholic,* 42 (Oct. 1977), p. 20

31   Noone, *Mary for Today,* p. 86

32   Mary Frances Shafer, "Accent," *Salt Magazine,* 8 (May 1982), p. 3

33   John represents the final redactor of the fourth gospel. Mary is mentioned twice in this gospel: at the marriage in Cana (John 2:1-12) and at the death on Calvary (John 19:25-27). The death of Jesus is the ultimate act of peacemaking. No explication of the Cana text is complete without inclusion of the Calvary text. For a concise current statement, see Michael O'Carroll, "Cana, the Wedding At" in *Theotokos: A Theological Encyclopedia of the Blessed Virgin Mary* (Wilmington, Del.: Michael Glazier, 1982), pp. 95-97

34   Max Thurian, *Mary: Mother of All Christians* (New York: Herder and Herder, 1964), pp. 118-119

35   The gospel is constructed on a plan of six liturgical feasts: three Passovers, one Pentecost, probably, a feast of Tabernacles and a feast of Dedication. *Ibid.,* p. 120

36   John McHugh, *The Mother of Jesus in the New Testament* (Garden City, N.Y.: Doubleday, 1975), pp. 396-397. Six signs are: (1) changing wtaer into wine, (2) healing ruler's son from 20 miles away, (3) curing poor cripple, immobile for 38 years; (4) feeding 5,000 from five loaves and two fishes; (5) giving sight to a man born blind; and (6) raising the dead Lazarus. The seventh sign, integral to the mystical pattern of wonders, transcends the previous six: the Resurrection

37   Thurian, *Mary: Mother of All Christians,* p. 119. For a more detailed plan, see Anchor Bible: *The Gospel According to John,* Raymond E. Brown (ed.) (Garden City: Doubleday, 1966), pp. cxl-cxli

38   Thurian, *Mary: Mother of All Christians,* p. 121. *The Gospel According to John,* Brown (ed.), p. 106

39   Thurian, *Mary: Mother of All Christians*, p. 120

40   *Ibid.*, p. 121 Ignace de la Potterie, "Mary and the Mystery of Cana: Abstract of 'La Madre di Gesù e il Misterio di Cana,' from *Civiltà Cattolica*, 130 (Dec. 1, 1979), p. 3107" in *Theology Digest*, 29 (Spring 1981), pp. 40-42. Concerning the ancient solar week which began on Wednesday, see *The Gospel According to John*, Brown (ed.), p. 106

41   Rosemary Ruether, *Mary, the Feminine Face of the Church* (Philadelphia: Westminster, 1977), p. 39. André Feuillet, "The Hour of Jesus and the Sign of Cana," *Johannine Studies* (Staten Island: Alba, 1964), pp. 17-37

42   Ruether, *Mary, the Feminine Face of the Church*, p. 39. See also Mary Anne Hoope, *Vineyard: An Ecclesiological Model* (unpublished dissertation, St. Louis University, 1981)

43   McHugh, *The Mother of Jesus in the New Testament*, p. 367

44   Feuillet, "The Hour of Jesus and the Sign of Cana," p. 35. Raymond Collins, "Mary in the Fourth Gospel: A Decade of Johannine Studies," *Louvain Studies*, 3 (Fall 1970), p. 125

45   McHugh, *The Mother of Jesus in the New Testament*, p. 363. I have used the literal English for the Semitism and the Greek, verse 4

46   *Ibid.*, p. 389. Also see Raymond Brown, "Roles of Women in the Fourth Gospel," *Theological Studies*, 36 (Dec. 1975), 695-696

47   McHugh, *The Mother of Jesus in the New Testament*, p. 389. For a complete literary analysis of the Greek, see pp. 462-466. See also Brown, "Roles of Women in the Fourth Gospel," pp. 695-696, n. 22 and n. 23. See also Gerhard Krodel, "The Mother of Jesus in the Gospel of John," *Mary in the New Testament: A Collaborative Assessment by Protestant and Roman Catholic Scholars*, Raymond Brown *et al.* (eds.) (Philadelphia: Fortress Press, 1978), pp. 182-186. Cana is probably Khirbet Qânâ, nine miles north of Nazareth. *The Gospel According to John*, Brown (ed.), p. 98

48   McHugh, *The Mother of Jesus in the New Testament*, pp. 389-390. A firkin is a British unit equal to about ¼ of a barrel. A barrel can hold 31-42 gallons.

49   *Ibid.*, p. 390

50   *Ibid.*, p. 391

51   Enigmatic phrase, "What is that . . . " is not to be explained in light of Old Testament parallels or of other Greek texts stemming from a Semitic background; rather it is an insertion by the evangelist, and a thoroughly Greek idiom, meaning, "Of what concern is it to me and to thee?" McHugh, *The Mother of Jesus in the New Testament*, p. 363. This very Semitic idiom expresses the relationship of these two human beings, in union or in opposition. Thurian, *Mary: Mother of All Christians*, p. 134. See also *The Gospel According to John*, Brown (ed.), p. 99, and H. Buck, "Redactions of the Fourth Gospel and the Mother of Jesus," *Studies in the New Testament and Early Christian Literature: Essays in Honor of A.P. Wikgren*, D.E. Aune (ed.) (Leiden: Brill, 1972), p. 177

52   Collins, "Mary in the Fourth Gospel: A Decade of Johannine Studies," p. 118 (1 Kings 17:18; 2 Kings 3:13; 2 Samuel 16:10, 19:23)

53   McHugh, *The Mother of Jesus in the New Testament*, p. 374

54   Thurian, *Mary: Mother of All Christians*, p. 134

55   Potterie, "Mary and the Mystery of Cana," p. 41. In saying that Cana is the "beginning" (archē)—not the "first"!—of Jesus' signs, John seems to be saying that Cana is an archetype, containing and prefiguring all that will follow.

56   Thurian, *Mary: Mother of All Christians*, p. 133. Concerning the faith of the disciples, see McHugh, *The Mother of Jesus in the New Testament*, p. 399

57   John 2:11. We are not told that his mother and disciples believed. Mary already had faith. McHugh, *The Mother of Jesus in the New Testament*, p. 399

58   Krodel, "The Mother of Jesus in the Gospel of John," p. 189. Brown, "Roles of Women in the Fourth Gospel," p. 697

59   McHugh, *The Mother of Jesus in the New Testament*, p. 394

60   On paradigms in history, see Gene Wise, *American Historical Explanations: A Strategy for Grounded Inquiry* (St. Paul: University of Minnesota Press, 1980). Patrick Bearsley, "Mary the Perfect Disciple: A Paradigm for Mariology," *Theological Studies*, 41 (Sept. 1980), pp. 461-504, is also useful

61   Usual festivities consisted of a procession in which the groom's friends brought the bride to his home, and then there was a wedding supper. Apparently the party lasted seven days (Judges 11-12, Tobias 11:19). The Mishnah ordained that the wedding of a virgin should take place on a Wednesday. *The Gospel According to John*, Brown (ed.), pp. 97-98

62   Rodriguez, "Peace (in the Bible)," p. 37

63   For extended explanation of Mary's queenship, see Firmin Schmidt, "The Universal Queenship of Mary," *Mariology*, Juniper Carol (ed.), vol. 2 (Milwaukee: Bruce, 1957), pp. 493-549, and William Behringer, "Queen of Peace," *Mary and the Beatitudes* (Staten Island: Alba, 1964), pp. 105-113

OUR LADY OF GUADALUPE: SYMBOL OF LIBERATION?
Mary DeCock, BVM

A serious investigation of Our Lady of Guadalupe as a religious symbol is appropriate at this time for both pastoral and scholarly reasons. Although Mexican in origin, the Guadalupan devotion is finding its way into the church in the United States where Mexican-Americans constitute a large part of the most rapidly growing segment in that church. Yet their religious culture is as foreign as their language to most North American Catholics. Since Guadalupan devotion differs significantly from the popular piety familiar to Catholics of European origin, it must be examined and understood if the church in the United States is to claim Mexican-Americans as its own. But, aside from these pastoral reasons, popular religion of which Guadalupan devotion is one form, is a legitimate object of inquiry in its own right.

In this chapter, therefore, I will briefly trace the origin and development of the Guadalupan tradition in Mexico, analyze the function of the Guadalupe symbol in Mexican culture, and describe the negative effects upon women which the tradition is claimed to have caused. I will then speculate on possible reinterpretations of the Guadalupe symbol by exploring insights from feminist and Latin American liberation theologians into Marian devotion in general and the Guadalupe event in particular. Finally, I will suggest a new direction for research that may help to preserve what I perceive as the real strength for women of Marian popular devotion.

Guadalupe in Historical Perspective

The origins of the Guadalupan tradition in Mexico date back to 1531, just a dozen years after Cortez "discovered" the resource-rich empire of the Aztecs and the *conquistadores* began their systematic effort to reclaim its lost treasures. The Franciscan missioners who arrived shortly after Cortez were at odds both with the barbaric tactics of the Spanish military and political authorities in the New World and with what appeared to them as the strange, savage religion of the natives. They were diligent in trying to destroy paganism, plant the true faith among the Aztecs, and establish a truly Christian church. In the midst of this church/state/native conflict, the transcendent religious experience we now know as the Guadalupan apparitions occurred.

There are many versions of the story and many variations in the details.[1] But the major events that structure the narrative are as clear as the interpretations are diverse. Juan Diego, a middle-aged Aztec and a recent convert to the Christian faith, set out one winter morning for mass at the monastery of Tlatololco. At the hill of Tepeyac where his ancestors had until recently worshipped their powerful goddess, Tonantzin, he was transfixed by the presence of a beautiful lady. She was surrounded by a cloud of transparent brightness and enveloped in a chorus of harmonious birdsong. At the sound of his own name, Juan approached her and heard this request:

> . . . it is my desire that a church be built here in this place for me, where, as your most merciful Mother and that of all people, I may show of my loving clemency, and the compassion that I bear to the Indians, and to those who love me and seek me, to all those who seek my protection, and call upon me in their travail and afflictions, and where I may hear their sorrows and prayers and give them consolation and help . . . go to the City of Mexico, to the palace of the Bishop who lives there to whom you will say that I have sent you, and that it is my pleasure that he build me a church in this place.[2]

Juan obeyed, and Fray Juan de Zumárraga, bishop-elect of Mexico, listened to the weary and frightened peasant with more than a touch of incredulity. Told to return on a later day, a disheartened Juan started home only to be greeted a second time by the woman he now recognized as the Virgin Mary and Mother of God. She repeated her request. He repeated his journey to the bishop. The still-skeptical Zumárraga demanded of Juan a sign from the Lady to assure him that it was truly the Mother of God who had sent him to request the building of a church.

Once again Juan began the long walk home and once again he was intercepted by the Lady, to whom he apologetically relayed the bishop's request for a sign. She told him—and he promised—to return the next day so that the sign might be delivered.

At home Juan Diego became involved in a family crisis. His uncle, Juan Bernardino, had suddenly contracted *cocliztli,* a deadly typhus fever, and he required Juan Diego's services for an entire day. Only 24 hours later as the nephew set out for the monastery to fetch a priest for his dying uncle did he remember his promise to the Mother of God. Frightened, he took another road to avoid her. But she encountered him, bade him not to worry about his uncle, whom she would care for, and sent him climbing to the tip of the barren Mexican hill to pick the roses that would be her response to the bishop. Now it was Juan's turn to be skeptical. But he did as he was told, discovered and picked a capeful of Castilian roses which the lady told him to conceal carefully until he presented them to the bishop in his palace. The world knows the rest of the story. The bishop received Juan reluctantly, but "gazed with wonder at the marvel of fresh roses and (a greater wonder still) the Holy Image which appeared painted on the cloak" as the flowers tumbled to the floor.

> . . . the height of Her sacred Image from the sole of Her foot to the top of Her head measures six hands, and one woman's hand. Her sacred face is very beautiful, grave, and somewhat dark; her precious body . . . is small; her hands are held at her breast; the girdle at her waist is violet; her right foot only shows, a very little, and her slipper is earthen in color; her robe is rose-colored; embroidered with various flowers outlined in gold; pendant at her throat is a little gold circlet which is outlined with a black line around it; in the middle it has a cross; and one discovers glimpses of another, inner vestment of white cotton daintily gathered at her wrists. The outer mantle which covers her from her head almost to her feet is of heavenly blue; halfway down its fullness hangs in folds, and it is bordered with gold, a rather wide band of gold thread, and all over it there are golden stars which are in number forty-six. Her most holy head is turned toward the right and is bending down; and on her

head above her mantle she wears a shining gold crown, and
at her feet there is the new moon with its horns pointed
upward; and exactly in the middle of it the Immaculate
Virgin is standing, and it would seem also, in the middle of
the sun, since its rays surround her everywhere. . . . This
divine Image as it is described stands above an angel . . .
and it seems as if he were very happy to be accompanying
the Queen of Heaven.[3]

Such was the Image the bishop saw. Giving thanks to the Mother of
God, he and his household knelt in contemplation before the Image and
went with Juan to Tepeyac where the Virgin had requested that a
church be built.

From Tepeyac Juan returned to his uncle's home to discover that Juan
Bernardino had been cured at the exact moment the Lady had promised.
Moreover, he had been honored by a visit from that same Lady and
informed that her Image should be called Santa Maria de Guadalupe.
Thus the fifth apparition of Mary was accompanied by a miracle of
healing, the first of many that were to come.

Zumárraga transferred the Image to the great church in the city of
Mexico where it remained until three years later when it was carried in
solemn procession and fiesta to the new Hermitage constructed at the
hill of Tepeyac. During the procession, a native, accidentally wounded
in the neck by a flying arrow, was healed when taken to the foot of the
Holy Image. The effect of the apparitions and the miracles upon the
native population was instantaneous and profound.

Mass baptisms took place on a scale such as the church has
scarcely seen. . . . Fray Toribia de Motolinia, whom the
Indians nicknamed "the Poor One," a generally reliable
witness, claims that nine million were baptized in that time
alone.[4]

Within a fortnight after the conquest, the improbable fusion of
Spanish Catholicism and Aztec religion, of European and Nahuatl
culture and blood, had been ratified by a heavenly intervention which is
a key element of Mexican life and culture to this day.

The question that concerns us here is not whether the apparition of
Mary to Juan occurred; obviously something took place that changed
not only attitudes but the course of history. Our question is the *meaning*

of Juan's experience. Virgilio Elizondo, contemporary Mexican-American scholar, interprets the apparitions as a conversion—for Juan Diego, a new sense of identity and human importance, a reinforcement of the Catholicism he had already espoused, and a firmer commitment to the church. For Zumárraga, the conversion was even more significant. A Spaniard, an educated cleric, a bishop-elect with authority from the king to challenge even the Audiencia (the civil authority of New Spain), Zumárraga listened to a simple, uneducated Indian, just two steps removed from paganism. He saw a beautiful image, the origin of which he could not explain. He changed his way of understanding the Mexican reality, of acting toward the Indian peoples. Zumárraga's experience forced him to step outside the philosophical framework in which he had been educated. Not scripture, not theology, but a transcendent experience merged the Christian and Aztec traditions, reversed and humanized Fray Juan de Zumárraga's relation to God, the church, and the Indians. That, for Elizondo, is the miracle.[5] Mary, in whatever form or fashion her impact occurred, was a mediator, an occasion for a human encounter that bridged class, race, and culture. As a result of that encounter, the two Juans became co-creators of a new world. A new vision of reality began to form.

Within that vision Mary too began to take on a new identity that made her part of a new race (Mexican) and an ancient culture (Aztec). In the minds of the natives, the Lady of Guadalupe not only represented Mary, the Mother of the Christian God with all the power she had acquired over the course of centuries. She also replaced Tonantzin, the fertility goddess of the Aztecs, and as such she inherited by association some of the powers and characteristics of her predecessor at Tepeyac. Mary was on her way to becoming a star in a new Sacred Canopy, a component of the "collective consciousness" that would characterize New Spain for centuries to come.[6] The Star had been launched from human experience, the most continuous and yet most enduring of all groundworks, and the devotion which it attracted was characterized by the exalted veneration from the two Juans, one Aztec and one Spanish, who called themselves "her sons."[7]

Time and space do not permit tracing the fascinating historical developments that have made the Lady of Guadalupe both a source of conflict and an integral symbol of today's Mexican and Mexican-

American culture. Religiously it is still a key element in the faith of millions; witness the hordes of pilgrims who visit the shrine each year. Pope John Paul II in his 1979 visit to Mexico was only the last in a long line of popes to pay special tribute to the famous Image. Psychologically, the effects of such Marian devotion have been considered both a flight into disastrous escapism from the real world and a motivating impulse for liberation.[8] Sociologically, the Guadalupan devotion has at various times united classes, cultures, races, sexes, and political parties, sometimes in admittedly uneasy alliances.[9]

The banner of Guadalupe has been carried by revolutionaries. Treaties of peace have been named for Guadalupe and signed in her basilica. Theologians have scoured scripture for references with which to bolster the religious significance of the apparitions.[10] Literary critics have mined the poetry and essays of the seventeenth and eighteenth centuries to document the evolution of the Guadalupan symbol in the Mexican national consciousness.[11] Scientists are still analyzing the texture of the maguey cloth on which the Image is printed and the quality of the paint, especially that of the eyes of the Image, where the reflections of Juan Diego and Zumárraga are thought to be reproduced.[12] Art historians have searched Aztec symbols for similarities to those of Guadalupe. Anthropologists have researched Aztec and Mayan legends and myths that seem to survive in the imported Spanish-Catholic devotion.[13] For every scholar who declares the apparition a fraud, another explicates the faith development of the people and the unceasing wonder the phenomenon provides.[14]

The devotion that began as a personal religious experience for a simple Indian peasant has taken on significance of amazing proportions. In the words of anthropologist Eric Wolfe, the Guadalupe symbol

> . . . links together family, politics, and religion; colonial past and independent present; Indian and Mexican. It reflects the salient social relationships of Mexican life, and embodies the emotions they generate. It provides a cultural idiom through which the tenor and emotions of these relationships can be expressed. It is, ultimately, a way of talking about Mexico: a collective representation of Mexican society.[15]

Today biblical scholars and theologians seek fresh ways to interpret the centuries-long devotion and to link them to new interpretations of Mary available from scripture. It is important that these new interpretations consider the functional aspects of Guadalupan devotion in Mexican culture as an integral part of their theologizing.

Guadalupe and the Oppression of Women

For a feminist the question is: How has Guadalupe—the all-pervasive symbol of Christian womanhood—affected the lives of women within its sphere of influence? At first glance the answer would seem to be "not at all."

Latin American women, like women in all countries, suffer a double denigration—both their work and their bodies are exploited. And the Catholic church gets a good share of the blame for sustaining both these types of oppression. Emphasis on woman's role as mother and child-nurturer may be intended by the church to underline the importance of the family, but in situations where women must work outside the home for the survival of themselves and their families such unrelieved emphasis is guilt-producing. Mexico, like other Latin American countries, has a high level of unemployment and underemployment.[16] As competition for jobs increases, women (whose salaries are always lower) get hiring preference. Unemployment among men increases even more quickly than the general norm. Women end up supporting their husbands financially. But the men in turn do not support their wives physically or psychologically by sharing the care of home and children. The church has not addressed these problems of women's work.

Still, discrimination against women in the workplace and within the household is not the greatest indignity that Latin American women suffer. Nor is the church's teaching on the key role of motherhood and family the prime target for critics of Our Lady of Guadalupe. Rather, it is the *idealization* by the church and society of both Mary and womanhood which is blamed for the denigration of women's sexuality.

Octavio Paz in his analysis of life and thought in Mexico speaks of woman as Enigma, an image of fecundity and death which both attracts and repels men.[17] Woman, he says, is at once "an idol, a goddess, a mother, a witch, or a muse . . . but she can never be her own self."[18] According to Paz, these contradictory aspects of womanhood are symbolized, on one hand, in Our Lady of Guadalupe, the ever Virgin Mother of God, the Queen of Heaven who spiritually consoles the poor, the weak and the oppressed. On the other hand, there is the *chingada* or violated mother, the *malinchista* who is even more passive than the virgin, does not reject violence but voluntarily gives herself to the world, losing her identity as she disappears into nothingness.

This dualistic vision of womanhood, Paz thinks, explains the enigma of male/female relationships in Mexico and accounts for the macho of males who display to women and the world an aggressiveness, invulnerability and insensitivity that mask a deep-seated inferiority. The female response which this macho demands is pure passivity, vulnerability, defenselessness against men and the exterior world.

Enrique Dussel, one of the few Latin American theologians of liberation who give serious consideration either to women or to the importance of Marian theology, offers basically the same functional interpretation: woman as passive victim of macho violence and social exploitation.[19] Dussel considers women's oppression within a threefold analytic of roles: the erotic or wife/husband relationship; the pedagogic or mother/child relationship; and the political or brother/sister relationship. For Dussel, the basic oppression of Latin women is erotic, originating with the violation of Indian women by Spanish conquistadors who appropriated them as concubines, used them as objects for sexual release, and superimposed upon them a patriarchal, patrilineal culture in place of the pre-conquest, Aztec matrilineal order where goddesses were first and outranked the father gods.

Today, Dussel asserts, erotic subjugation still occurs in Latin America through well-defined female roles: (1) the wife's obligation to satisfy her husband's sexual desires in marriage; (2) her auxiliary role to him as housekeeper, and (3) her charge as exclusive educator for their children. The mystique of women who strive to fulfill these triple roles perfectly is sustained through the female "virtues" of passivity and dependence. Woman is a sexually "closed" and unresponsive object for her sexual partner. But Mary, the Virgin of Guadalupe, whom Dussel considers the symbol of free and loving womanhood, has no relevance as a symbol of erotic love relationships. Mary's freedom appears to be freedom *from* sexuality. She opened herself to the Word of God and to motherhood in faith. She became the spouse of Joseph, sister to her sisters, mother of Jesus, teacher of her son, protector of the nascent church.[20] She is a symbol of the parent/child and sister/brother roles. For the erotic female symbol Dussel looks to the Song of Songs. He sees Mary as a symbol of sexlessness.

Under the rubrics of cultural analysis Guadalupismo, the devotion or cult of Mary, is the expression of religion as the sexual and psychological domination of women. Unlike Tonantzin, the Aztec goddess whose attributes she somewhat shares, Mary is not the autonomous Earth Mother and creator. The Virgin Mother of God, dogmatically defined by the church only in relation to her son, is a cultural symbol of Otherness—unworldly, passive, sexless, a model of abstract purity. Mary's role as mediator positions her as merciful, compassionate, an effective intercessor with her son whose human sufferings are also a key factor in Latin American devotion. But her power is a power of petition and dependence. In the macho culture nourished by devotion to the Virgin Mother, every man honors his own physical mother as the pure unviolated woman; his bride must come to him virginal and undefiled. But all other women are considered weak, seductive, unworthy of trust. For males, the *mala mujer* resides close to the surface of every female Latin American consciousness. After marriage, the once-pure bride may not travel alone, make independent decisions, converse with men other than her husband. Like the antebellum southern lady in the United States, she is confined to a mythical pedestal similar to that of the Mother of God whom she venerates. There, safe in her dependence, she observes a society which excuses male promiscuity, practical polygamy, wife-beating, and deception. Meanwhile, she assumes her responsibilities as servant to her husband's needs and career, and homemaker and educator for their children. Or as breadwinner for them in the absence of her spouse. Clearly the Guadalupe symbol has carried a mixed message to Latin Americans.

For the Christian feminist it is a depressing thought that Catholicism's exemplary cultural symbol of womanhood has been so narrowly described, rigidly defined, and mythically exalted by males that she cannot symbolize the three-fold levels of liberation which North American feminist and Latin American theologies demand: a freedom at once personal, political, and spiritual. The choice women must face is either to look beyond Mary for other examples of independent Christian womanhood or to attempt to liberate the symbol itself.

Problems of Symbolic Reinterpretation

Symbols, of course, are not mere signs that can be reoriented easily or at will. Symbols emerge; they are not constructed. Their power lies in the fact that they are ambiguous, developed over time by living praxis. They link, in their own nonlogical way, patterns of behavior, modes of thought, attitudes, values both personal and political.[21] Historically the Guadalupe symbol has functioned to unify races, classes, and sexes against oppression. It has always been a revolutionary symbol. In the sixteenth century the apparition revolutionized the church in New Spain by integrating mestizos, Indians, and Creoles into its aristocratic Spanish membership. In the early nineteenth century, liberal Mexican Catholics rallied behind the Guadalupe banner to initiate Mexico's independence from Spain. In the later nineteenth century, Guadalupe helped unify Zapata's peasant revolt. Aware of the national importance of the symbol, the revolutionary socialist government of Mexico today helps finance the Basilica of Guadalupe while the national constitution prohibits political activity by the church. Thus, Mexico officially recognizes the subversive power lurking behind the lovely religious image.

But the ambiguity of the Guadalupe symbol is dramatized by the fact that while it has supported political freedom it has also sustained personal oppression. Women honor its historically liberating record unaware that subliminally it has been used against them. The feminist question now becomes: can we liberate this basically religious symbol of its macho Mexican nationalism or must we forget it and move on to more direct strategies of change?

Andres Guererro, a Mexican-American advocate of symbolic reinterpretation, says that the symbol will become effectively liberating when a prophet arises to help the oppressed confront the injustices in their lives. Thus women bonding together to confront their own situations will alter the symbolic meaning as they change the oppressive realities. But the process of change is dialectical. Scholars who explore the ambi-

guity of symbols bring new understandings of reality to the consciousness of the group. Liberation theologians who recapture hidden dimensions of folk religion and cultic devotion open up new expressions of
faith to the entire community.[23] When scripture scholar Elisabeth
Schüssler Fiorenza offers fresh profiles of gospel women, or theologian
Rosemary Radford Ruether resurrects from the "usable past" of tradition a new model of female leadership, contemporary readers begin to
identify in a different way with the Christian sisters and foresisters.
Symbolic reinterpretations mediate new self-concepts; new-found
identities facilitate involvement in action for social change. New wine
strains old skins. New social forms emerge side by side with developing
new worldviews. Whatever the dialectic, life precedes dogma as well as
law.

But bringing together the experiences of the ordinary Christian
people, the liberating aspects of the gospel and Christian tradition, and
the liberating dimensions of popular devotion is a task of momentous
proportions. A close look at the Puebla documents demonstrates the
complications of the problem. One of the liberating thrusts of Vatican
II was to re-evangelize the common folk of Latin America and the world
to the central importance of Christological concepts and sacramental
rituals. By design the eucharist and rites of reconciliation nudged exag-
gerated, often superstitious Mary devotion into the background. In
Mexico, Mary's altars were moved to the back of the churches (if not to
the back yard). But popular devotion to her persisted by way of little
shrines in the kitchen, by the roadside, on the dashboard.

Twenty years after Vatican II, the Puebla documents both praise
Marian devotion and herald the human values of folk Catholicism including Guadalupan piety. Yet the documents offer no help in determining what the human values of the traditional devotion might be.
Every Marian title which the church has ever used is now appropriated
to the Virgin of Guadalupe whom the Puebla documents call Queen of
the Americas. Theologically, Mary is treated as model of the church
(282-303). Women (834-839) and popular religion (460-468) both
appear as a focus for evangelization. Social justice is grounded in anthropology (472-479), but the oppression of women as a matter of
injustice is cited merely as a footnote (1135). A theology of liberation
developed solely out of the Puebla documents cannot free women. If

Latin American women are to claim Our Lady of Guadalupe as a symbol of their liberation, they themselves will need to discover how it can "illuminate and disclose meaning in new, unexpected ways that speak to new experiential needs."[24] So too, if the popular devotion to Guadalupe is to find roots in the liberating strands of the Christian tradition, something more than the mere elaboration of historic Marian titles must be found. To this end, it is useful to examine recent theological reinterpretations of Mary that have already been offered by scholars in North and Central America.

Recent Interpretations of Mary

Feminist and liberation theologians are alike in their stress on holistic liberation. They demand a model of person adequate to human self-development. They call for self-determination in the political order (which for feminists means equality in the home and church as well as in the workplace). They aspire to spiritual liberation involving a new cosmovision that situates the new man (and the new woman) within the new church and the new earth. What have these theologians to say about Mary as a model of liberated womanhood?

According to Virgilio Elizondo, the entire Guadalupan legend is liberating. For him, Mary is a prophet of freedom and responsibility for all.[25] He views her encounter with the angel of the annunciation as her "peak experience"—a *mysterium tremendum*. He *says* that Mary is active and totally involved, but he sees her destiny as already settled at the moment of her peak experience, a destiny of total involvement in the work of her son. Nor does he document this involvement; rather, he pictures Mary as living out her lift under a "veil of faith,"[26] never understanding what was going on in her son's life though completely supportive of his work. In other words, Mary is a woman who "never tries to steal the show, but is always *in her proper place* cooperating with her son in the salvation of the world"[27] (italics mine). Mary's prophetic witness is pictured not as active but as passive. There is no hint that Mary may have struggled to life the veil of faith, no evidence that she grew in comprehension of Jesus' mission as she "pondered in her heart."

To give him his due, Elizondo tries to be sensitive to the oppression of women. He endeavors to rescue both the liberating aspects of the Guadalupe symbol and legitimate devotion to Mary. His vision of the new church is an ideal feminists can share. He is attentive to the aspects of Indian culture which surround the Guadalupan devotion—the music, the flowers, the color, the emotion, the intuition, the ritual, the story— all those aspects of the folk festivals where Guadalupan piety still appears. These are the stuff of popular religion and the cultural ingredients that lend themselves to exploration from a feminist perspective. Unfortunately, Elizondo does not use them so. Instead he refers to other popular religious practices such as rosaries and novenas as "gimmicks" and superficial devotion.[28] And he contrasts Mary and her openness with Eve who was closed unto herself, refusing to "surrender herself . . . ushering in the reign of selfishness, egoism and death to the world."[29] Elizondo has yet to come to terms with the basic male/female dualism that undergirds sexism for Dussell, Ruether *et. al.,* and with the polar images of women in theology and in Mexican culture.

Elizondo treats Mary as prophet. Scripture scholar Raymond Brown sees her as disciple. The liberating principle of discipleship is his starting point for a theology of Mary that reinforces devotion to Our Lady of Guadalupe. Basing his argument on the gospel of Luke, Brown draws a picture of Mary who, doing the will of God, becomes the "first Christian disciple."[30] The disciple Mary rejoices because "God her savior . . . has regarded the low estate of his slave woman." For Brown, the event of Mary's motherhood means discipleship because in her God has put down the mighty and exalted the lowly—an insight essentially the same as that expressed by Jesus, who proclaimed, "Blessed are you who are poor. . . . Blessed are you who are hungry and persecuted; woe to you who are rich."

The link between the Mary of scripture and the Lady of Guadalupe lies in this understanding and proclamation of the word "in terms of the life of the poor and the slaves of whom she was a representative."[31] For the downtrodden Indians of sixteenth-century Mexico, the apparition of Mary in the "ancient garb of the mother of the Indian gods [who] promises to show forth love and compassion, defense and help" was a true message of hope to the oppressed. The devotion of the Indians to Our Lady, then, "constituted an authentic development of the Gospel of discipleship."[32]

The interpretation of discipleship as liberating is attractive. But it does not speak to women as human persons seeking liberation in their intimate and familial relationships. Brown is concerned with political liberation. And, as Elisabeth Schüssler Fiorenza reminds us, the Guadalupe symbol already has a good political record. Men have fought for political freedom under the banner of Guadalupe, but they have continued to oppress wives, daughters, and granddaughters. In fact, used to legitimate war and nationalism, the Guadalupe symbol has actually reinforced macho violence.

The inadequacy of Brown's concept of discipleship becomes clear when one considers the nature of liberation theology. As a reflection on reality, liberating theology arises out of commitment and involvement in liberating action.[33] Reflection on the lives of women, by women working for their own liberation, leads to discovering new ways of "interpreting" the stories of scripture. The gospels have no specific norm *vis a vis* women or any other particular group. Jesus' mode of theologizing was to make a judgment relative to the humanness of each situation, not to apply a predetermined theological principle.[34] This accounts for his conflict with the Pharisees. So, Brown's interpretation of the annunciation and the Magnificat as a principle of discipleship is not of itself liberating. Discipleship is a nonliberating concept insofar as the church carefully limits certain classes of actions (ordination, administration of some sacraments) to certain classes of disciples (male). But Mary's judgment on her own condition, her reflection on her own slave status (he has regarded the humility of his handmaid . . . he has done great things for me), shows Mary herself thinking as a liberation theologian! Following her example, then, women are practicing, liberating disciples insofar as they are critical of unjust norms. They are practicing disciples when they criticize the patriarchalism in the church, when they expose its scriptural, institutional, and theological modes of oppression, when they act to free themselves from the unjust limitations imposed upon them by their religious heritage. But liberation is in the process, not in the principle.

For Brown, Mary exhibited the qualities of a disciple—unwavering faith, obedience, and love for the poor. But the real liberation she offered the Indians by her dark-skinned image was her prophetic critique of the racism in the church. The image of Santa Maria de Guadalupe—

mediator, evangelist, prophet, disciple, and theologian—was also that of a young pregnant woman, clearly identified by her garments with the dignity and power of a conquered nation. She is a symbol women can identify with today in their slave status within the family, society, and church. She offers them a critique of their historic sexism.

Andres Guererro finds Our Lady of Guadalupe under her title, Mother of Mexico, a truly liberating symbol. For Mexicans and Chicanos, Guererro says, Mary is first and foremost a mother and a mediatrix, not a wife, companion, daughter, or sister. In her presence, Mexicans envision themselves as children before a "strong, symbolic spiritual mother always there to lend a helping hand to the poor."[35] Just as her physical darkness spells acceptance of the brown, mestizo skin most typical of rural life, so the songs and the fiestas that honor her convey the warmth and affection which her children feel toward her. In a culture where women are frequently heads of families, the concept of Our Lady of Guadalupe as mother is not at all patriarchal. It is a recognition of woman as the nucleus of culture. Motherhood is of the very "essence of Chicano consciousness." At this point Guererro's theology takes a fascinating turn.

Macho, he reminds us, is a Spanish word which found its way into Mexican culture at the time of the conquest when Spanish encomenderos brought their sexual violence to bear upon Indian women. Since that time, *la malinche* (the title given to Doña Marina, the mistress of Cortez) has been a synonym for traitor and an epithet applied to women in scorn and derision. For Guererro, the Lady of Guadalupe is a symbol, not of idealized Christian womanhood, but of the unviolated Aztec woman who is also mother, a symbol of hope and survival for women and for all Indians. He sees the violated *la malinche* as a symbol of woman's struggle for survival in the face of unprecedented Spanish male violence.[36] The fact that Mexican men blamed *la malinche* for her own rape was a function of their own impotence before the foreign conquerers, a cowardice men still mask behind their macho image.

Guadalupe, then, is a symbol of liberation for both men and women because she stands against the violence men adopt to hide their fears and by which they assault women's personhood in so many ways. His concern about sexual oppression and its relation to the veneration of Guadalupe comes to terms with a major problem of Marian devotion.

But once again, the liberation he suggests is liberation of women by men who are at the same time liberating themselves and their culture. Women, he agrees, must liberate themselves. So he intentionally opens the question of the role of women and the process of liberation in which they are now engaged in order to achieve their own dignity and equality.

> Women as specific victims in every culture hold a special place and have a very important mission in announcing their liberation. Guadalupe can be used as a powerful symbol of liberation by women themselves.[37]

Through interviews with Chicano women, Guererro tries to discover women's feeling toward Guadalupe and their own liberation.[38] Only women actually interpreted the importance of the Guadalupe symbol in terms of faith, he tells us. For Lupe Anguiano, the Lady of Guadalupe stands as a symbol of "the importance of ourselves as human beings." By strengthening faith in self, Guadalupe strengthens one's faith in Christ, in God, and in the church.

Dolores Huerta, co-worker with labor organizer Cesar Chavez, points out that for Chicanos it is frequently the mother, not the father, who is present as head of the family. Despite the misuses of the symbol, Huerta says, Mexican women and all the poor can claim Mary as symbol of motherhood because they have the existential human faith experience that "mother is and always will be there." Moreover, it is the overtones of the miraculous surrounding the devotion which provide for Huerta the dimensions of social liberation that Guadalupe represents for her. It is through the power of that symbol that the poor have faith that they *can* overcome. The motherhood Huerta refers to is no mere biological fact; it is a social reality of strength in the face of human suffering.

One further insight into the way Latin American women themselves relate to Mary comes from Ernesto Cardenal's *Gospel of Solentiname*. Cardenal's book is essentially a transcript of comments on scripture readings made by his campesino parishioners in the base community on the Island of Solentiname in Lake Nicaragua. A careful reading of the comments on scripture passages treating of Mary reveals some interesting trends. Women respond to different themes than do men.

In the story of the annunciation Ernesto himself translates the opening phrases of the Hail Mary as "I congratulate you, God-favored one."[39] The campesino Tomás comments on Mary's reaction to the greeting as one of fear, the "natural reaction of the poor" when asked to be important. Marcelino commiserates with Mary's questioning of the message because she had been "deprived of a husband." But Natalia summarizes the situation very simply: Mary was a woman of the people like us, and Jesus was the son of Mary and of love. Natalia sees no fear, no deprivation, no self-pity.

Reflecting on Matthew 1:18-25, only Teresita looks at the situation of Mary in a story where Joseph (in dialog with the angel) is the main character. Mary is a "good woman," she tells her companions as they discuss Joseph as a man of faith.[40] Commenting on Luke 1:45-55, the women reveal the fact that the campesinos carry the verses of the Magnificat as an amulet (a form of popular religion with overtones of magic).[41] They notice that Mary referred to herself as a "slave," and that a slave to God is one who is there to serve others, to liberate them and bring them freedom.[42] They see Mary as happy because she is a liberator like her son, and because she understood him (like themselves, who watched their sons go off to the revolution as guerrillas) and did not oppose his prophetic mission. They see her as poor and humble because she is herself liberated by God, as a woman who sang about equality and a society without social classes, as a woman whom Herod would call a communist![43]

This limited analysis of comments by Latin women is hardly a base on which to build a feminist theology. But it does indicate that Latin women identify with Mary differently and more frequently than do males, and that the campesino women envision her not merely as a powerful queen or mediator, not as an ideal and virgin mother who works miracles, but as a simple and poor woman like themselves, one in sympathy with their own aspirations for dignity, freedom, and equality. Their comments on scripture merge people's religion with the Word of God at the most fundamental level, that of their own experience as women.

Not surprisingly, North American feminist theologian Rosemary Radford Ruether has provided a better interpretation of Mary as autonomous woman than have any of the Latin American liberationists. She reminds us that interpretations of the annunciation story usually have portrayed Mary as passive recipient of the Word, acting in obedience to the Spirit of the Lord for whom she was an instrument in the designs of providence. But that interpretation is limited. Luke makes Mary a central figure in the annunciation story where she appears as a self-directed person. Visited by an angel, she is

> consulted in advance and gives her consent; thus she becomes an active, personal agent in the drama of God's incarnation. She goes to visit her cousin Elizabeth on her own initiative. At no time in these two events does she ask permission from her husband-to-be. . . .
>
> Luke makes Mary an active participant in the drama of Jesus' birth, accepting it through an act of free consent, and meditating upon the meaning of his future mission. Thus, Luke begins that tradition which transforms Mary from being merely the historical mother of Jesus into an independent agent cooperating with God in the redemption of humanity. In other words, she becomes a theological agent in her own right.[44]

In the Magnificat, Ruether continues, Mary "proclaims herself as the embodiment of Israel. . . . She is the initial agent in the unfolding of a divine revolution in history." Furthermore, Ruether points out, although Mary is presented as a virgin in the gospels, her virginity and the virgin birth of her son are statements about Jesus' divine chosenness, not assertions about Mary's body per se.[45] Mary emerges from the "infancy narratives" as an actor in command of her own choices, including the disposition of her own body.

But, taken as a whole, the gospels do not picture Mary as an unwavering disciple of her son during his ministry. Three of the four gospels speak of Jesus' family as unresponsive to his teaching when he spoke in the area near his home (Matthew 13:54-58; Mark 6:1-6; Luke 4:14-30). Mark records an incident where Jesus' family, thinking that he was "beside himself," tried to seize him and bring him home to Nazareth (Mark 3:20-35). With varying grades of "distance-ing," Luke, Matthew and Mark all show Jesus as asserting the superiority of discipleship over family relationships; Mark suggests an outright rejection by Jesus of his mother and family. John pictures Mary at Cana as failing to understand the meaning of her son's mission and words (John 2:1-11). And only John explicitly lists Mary, the mother of Jesus, among those women present at his crucifixion (John 19:25). If Mary was among the disciples of Jesus during his lifetime, that fact is thinly documented by gospel accounts of Jesus' ministry.[46]

Ruether concludes that the Mary of scripture is a "conventional" woman, not a model for the liberated woman. Mary's theological significance lies in her usefulness as an eschatological symbol for the new humanity and for the church.[47]

Toward a New Popular Symbol

As the previous survey of recent Marian scholarship has shown, the theological task of "liberating" the Guadalupe symbol is a formidable one. Very few Latin American liberation theologians deal with sexism and the oppression of women; the personal autonomy of wives and mothers, the equality of partners in marriage are simply not on their agenda. Feminist theologians are not dealing with themes specifically relevant to the Guadalupan tradition which is marginal to their North American experience. They are concerned about the roles and significance of *all* women in scriptures and the church, and they tend to interpret Mary as an ecclesial symbol. For them, Mary Magdalene emerges as a better model of personal liberation than does the ever-virgin Mary.[48]

Moreover, the task will require the combined talents and energies of many women for a long time to come. Latin American women themselves must examine their own experiences and their particular forms of oppression; they must also discover what are the freedom-sustaining dimensions of the popular Guadalupan tradition which are meaningful to them. But scripture scholars, theologians, and historians must assist them in grounding both of these in scripture and tradition to justify the fresh feminist interpretations as well-founded developments, not innovations. It is in these latter areas (perhaps only in these areas) that North American feminists can assist their Mexican sisters.[49]

As a result of my investigations, I would like to propose a line of inquiry and reflection which might begin to address the problems of reinterpretation as I have come to understand them. The process would mean attempting to envision Mary living out her life in history as an ordinary Jewish mother, operating within the givens of her biological and racial inheritance, the social status, role expectations, family and community relationships which provided the context within which her choices would have been made. Both scriptural and historical resources for this task are meager, so what I propose is a very meager beginning.[50]

Let us assume with the feminist scholars that the Bible gives a limited view of history. Marian references in the texts are few. The texts of both testaments are written by males; they reflect, if not social realities, at least a type of society that males envisioned as good and desirable. Scriptural legal codes indicate that enough freedom for women existed to make the laws necessary, so we cannot be sure just what actual conditions of male/female interactions existed in Jewish society at the beginning of the Christian era.[51]

Let us assume, too, with proponents for liberation of women in the United States, that self-liberation means personal autonomy. That is, a strong sense of one's own identity and personhood, the courage to make choices and live with the consequences. Let us assume that maturity and self-confidence are a necessary base for reciprocity and mutuality in heterosexual human relationships, that such human exchanges cannot flourish in an atmosphere of domination and dependency. Given these assumptions, let us engage our historical imaginations in re-creating what the process of liberation might have meant to a Jewish mother in Mary's day.

By her birth the Jewish woman was bound to a particular time in history with all its particular laws and customs, traditions and cultural restrictions. According to the legal codes of the Hebrews, women were considered unclean, in need of purification because of their bodily functions of menstruation and child-bearing. They were expected to bear children for their husbands (to be barren was a curse), but after child-bearing they were also expected to present themselves for a ritual purification that made them clean once more. And the purification ceremony was more rigid following the birth of girl babies than that of boys (Leviticus 12).

Secondly, if we can judge by the frequency of images in the Old Testament, women were widely thought of as seducers and temptresses. The favorite symbol of Israel's unfaithfulness to Yahweh was that of a harlot. The legal punishment for women fornicators or adulterers was death—a harsher punishment that that for their male partners.

Finally, in Mary's day women were considered the property of men. The ninth commandment as conveyed through the Baltimore catechism is less familiar to us in the Exodus version: "Thou shalt not covet thy neighbor's wife, nor his servant, nor his ox, nor his ass, nor any other thing that is his" (Exodus 20:17). Jewish women were married to men under circumstances arranged by their fathers and brothers. Status came through the male line. If a woman were widowed, she became the legal property of her brother-in-law, expected to bear children for the patriarchal family to which she now belonged. These are the cultural restrictions within which a woman in Mary's time would have grown to adulthood. Read with this particular context in mind, what do the scriptures tell us about Mary?

We can presume that Mary would have been reared by her parents to know and respect the roles and rituals which affected women. As a faithful Jew, she would have been taught the importance of becoming a good, obedient wife and mother, one faithful to Yahweh and to the traditions of her people.

Mary seems to have been a person of uncertain lineage not clearly connected to either the Davidic or Levite families to which her son is linked. For reasons of his own, Matthew listed her in his geneology of Jesus with Tamar, Rehab, Ruth and Bethsheba—all women with some marital irregularities in their lives, three of them non-Jewish.[52] The evangelists sometimes referred to the son Mary bore as "son of Joseph," sometimes as "son of Mary."[53] A hint of illegitimacy lurks both in scripture and in the apocrypha to indicate that rumors were part of the burden Mary carried with her for many years. She had listened to the message of the angel and responded to it by saying "Yes, I will become a mother even though I do not yet have a husband." Her betrothal suggests that she was old enough to know what the consequences of her decision might be. Choice is self defining. Mary made a hard one—a first step toward discipleship, but only a first step.

Mary then decided to visit her cousin Elizabeth who was also pregnant under some unusual, although not scandalous, circumstances. She seems to have made a solitary journey into the hill country, leaving

Joseph, her troubled husband-to-be, at home in Nazareth. It was in the exchange of rather stylized Jewish greetings (antiphons) that Mary is said to have sung her Magnificat, a statement redolent of the prophetic tradition and one sophisticated enough that Luke must have envisioned her as knowledgeable in Hebrew scriptures. Here, in solidarity with her cousin—in a situation of Jewish sisterhood—Mary made a statement the Nicaraguan women of Solentiname say would merit her the epithet "communist." No matter that Luke put the words into her mouth; whatever his theological intentions, we can see Mary's Magnificat defining in advance the prophetic mission her son was to carry out in accordance with the will of Yahweh whom he would call "father" and image as mother![54] Scholars tell us that Jesus' understanding of himself as Messiah developed as he grew. Isn't it likely that Mary helped the young Jesus come to understand the meaning of the prophetic tradition he grew up to represent?

We know that Mary was faithful to patriarchal Jewish customs. Luke tells us that she and Joseph presented Jesus in the temple and gave an offering, that Mary participated in the purification rites of the day. With Joseph's help she protected the child from danger; their status as members of an oppressed minority within the Roman empire required a long trip to Egypt to save their son's life. When they lost him in the Temple at Jerusalem, Mary scolded her son a bit for taking on a role she did not understand. Allow her a human reaction. There is nothing in the words "pondering in her heart" to suggest that she *always* meditated lovingly on the Father's will that Jesus spoke about.[55] She may have worried that Jesus was becoming a prophet too quickly, or wished that she and Joseph had left him at home! Later, when Jesus was ready to launch out on his own, Mary confronted him with an embarrassing shortage of wine at a wedding feast they were attending. Why must we insist on *not* hearing the note of formality (rejection?) that John put into Jesus' words to his mother at Cana?[56] It is the same impersonal note that Mark records when Jesus' family tried to take him back to Galilee because he was "beside himself." Isn't it just possible, remembering the variant traditions that circulated in the early centuries of the church, that Mary was worried about her son, confused about his answers and actions, but (as the peasant woman in Nicaragua sug-

gested) liberated enough to let him go his own way—even liberated
enough to choose *not* to follow him as yet?

By the time of Jesus' adulthood, tradition still holding, Mary should
have been about 45 years old and a widow. Widows, we are told, were
paradigms of poverty in the Jewish tradition.[57] Yet, there is no indica-
tion that during his public ministry Jesus treated Mary with the special
care and concern he gave to other women known to be his followers. He
cured no issue of blood for her. If a rumor of adultery still circulated
among the village gossips, Jesus is not known to have quelled it. There
is no word of praise that Mary had sat at his feet while another took care
of the kitchen. Yet John clearly places Mary at the foot of her son's cross
where she was asked to take on yet another son. Let us remember that
Mary *accepted* her son's beloved disciple, as much as Jesus bequeathed
his friend to her. Perhaps that acceptance was the big step in Mary's discipleship.

The scriptures agree that Mary was one of the followers at Pentecost.
And tradition describes them as a motley crew. The worldly, converted
and loving Magdalene, the cowardly Peter, the ambitious sons of Zebe-
dee, and the brothers of Jesus—all of them had missed the meaning of
discipleship before the resurrection. Perhaps Mary became liberated
enough to accept her son's friends and his message at the very time this
group was about to become the subversives her Magnificat had profiled
30 years earlier. A typical Jewish mother of her day, conditioned by her
culture, subject to a traditional role, educated to Yahweh's love for the
poor, Mary seems slowly to have liberated herself from Jewish religious
conservatism.

According to some scholars, the possibility that Mary bore other children after the birth of Jesus is clearly referred to in Scripture and tradition,[58] and suggests a personal and intimate relationship between Mary
and Joseph. But the potential of Mary as a symbol for liberation within
marriage which that relationship might suggest is probably lost beyond
redemption for Catholics committed to the doctrinal emphasis on
Mary's status as ever-virgin. Nevertheless, to observe Mary's personal
movement from Jewish mother to belated public figure among Jesus'
disciples is to perceive in her a human dimension that Catholic Mariology lacks and ignores. Mary coping with a lifetime of family conflict,
struggling to understand a controversial son, facing his critics; Mary

coming to terms with a religious renewal movement that called into question some of her lifelong traditions and customs even as it brought new meaning to others; Mary casting her lot with Jesus at the moment his male disciples deserted him—here is a model of developing discipleship that contemporary women can understand.[59] It is a model not too different from the interpretation of Mary offered by the campesino women of Solentiname.

Conclusion

Despite the emphasis placed on theology by the official church, popular religion has always held its own in history. Its strength lies in its origin in the human condition with its joys and sufferings, peak experiences and moments of despair. Common folk, like theologians and scripture scholars, look to their ancestors and their traditions, to culture and to religion in an effort to make sense out of the complications of life. And somehow they sustain a deep-seated hope that they can transcend today and create a better tomorrow. But their criteria for religious adequacy are not the internal coherence of a logical argument or the proportionality of conceptual relationships within a focus of meaning.[60] Their criteria are much more simple: does the religious devotion satisfy a human need? Does it express a human emotion? Does it fit a particular situation?

Cultic devotion to Mary may indeed be a mixture of what psychologists call escapism and Christians call faith. The Guadalupan symbol is ambiguous, oppressing, liberating, and enduring. Through it Mexican women venerate the virgin Mary and admire her as Queen. But they also identify with and are strengthened by the human dimensions of Mary that Guadalupe symbolizes for them. Her image came to them, not as an unmarried virgin, but as that of a Lady, a title given to the wife of the Viceroy. She is alone, young, pregnant, beautiful, with compassionate eyes and the ancestral dress of an Aztec princess. For centuries the common folk of the pre-patriarchal church, the peasant women of the middle ages, the pueblas of Mexico and the fishing villages of Nicaragua have found in Mary some sort of personal symbol that the theologians have missed. It is this something that keeps them appealing to her for safe pregnancies, healthy babies, economic windfalls, and political victories. But these human qualities of Mary are not accessible in Marian theology as we have it today.

The gospels are theological statements about Jesus, the son of God, who is God. Popular devotion does not question that. If it errs toward belief in the divine, it is by exaggeration, not by devaluation. But popular devotion speaks very directly to the particular experiences of people in history, and it has an uncanny way of getting behind the theology of the gospel-writers to the human condition out of which the gospel stories developed in the first place.

Elisabeth Schüssler Fiorenza suggests that feminist scholars must develop a new critical biblical hermeneutic and fresh historical reconstructions before they can understand the role of women in the Christian tradition. They must attempt to see the Jesus movement within its Jewish religious context and try to recapture the critical feminist impulse existing *within* the patriarchal tradition.[61] On those terms the reconstruction of a profile of Mary as a Jewish mother gradually becoming a disciple within the Jesus movement may be difficult and long-coming. History and scripture studies are simply not adequate to the task at present. But popular religious devotion does not bear this burden. People hear the gospel stories from the point of view of their own historical predicament. Mary represents to them the fullness of personhood, a paradigm of human goodness whose universality transcends time, sex, race, and nationality. Devotions and symbols such as the Lady of Guadalupe are the mediating rituals by which the universal becomes a concrete particular—a guide for behavior, a hope for tomorrow, the courage to keep on going a little longer. They are the mechanisms of theological reflection for those whose scholarship comes through the school of hard knocks and common sense.

If the Guadalupe symbol still holds some power of liberating hope for women, perhaps this is because it has largely escaped sophisticated theological analysis. If reinterpreting it means harnessing it to the sexist perspective of existing male theology and scripture scholarship, the unlettered peasant women of Mexico will be further deprived by the evangelization which the Puebla documents prescribe for them. But, if the reinterpretation could mean relating it to a fresh, holistic, human hermeneutic, a more down-to-earth mode of theologizing, not only women but the entire church and even the gospel would benefit. Let us hope for the latter.

Footnotes

1   Like the gospels, the basic accounts of the Guadalupan apparitions were written well after the events and reflect the authors' points of view. The oldest account (called Nican Mopohua from its first words) seems to have been written in the Nahuatl language by an Aztec scholar, Antonio Valeriano, about 20 years after the apparitions. The earliest account in Spanish (1648) is a theological reflection by Miguel Sanchez, a Mexican bachiller. The Spanish account by Lazo de la Vega (1649) is a translation based on Valeriano's mms. The narrative by Luis Bercerra Tanco (1675) explicitly stresses the apparition as a sign of compassion to the Indians.

2   Luis Becerra Tanco, "The Felicity of Mexico in the Wonderful Apparition of the Virgin Mary, Our Lady of Guadalupe (1648)," in *Dark Virgin: The Book of Our Lady of Guadalupe,* Donald Demarest and Coley Taylor (eds.) (Freeport, Maine: Coley Taylor, Inc., 1956), p. 101

3   Luis Lazo de la Vega, "The Miraculous Apparition of the Beloved Virgin Mary, Our Lady of Guadalupe, at Tepeyacac, near Mexico City (1649)," in *Dark Virgin,* p. 52. Tepeyacac is an alternate spelling for Tepeyac, the spelling used in this paper.

4   *Dark Virgin,* p. 9.

5   See Virgilio Elizondo, *La Morenita: Evangelizer of the Americas* (San Antonio, Texas: Mexican American Cultural Center, 1980), and *Galilean Journey: The Mexican-American Promise* (Maryknoll, New York: Orbis Books, 1983) for complete developments of this thesis.

6   Peter Berger, *The Sacred Canopy* (New York: Doubleday & Co., 1967). According to Berger's sociological theory, religious symbols both derive their legitimacy from human experience and legitimate the societal stuctures and subjective personal identities of those whose lives they help to socialize. Occurring as it did at the beginning of the development of New Spain, the Guadalupan phenomenon would become a powerful cultural symbol regardless of the fact that its religious meaning was controversial. In fact, its very ambiguity would add to its potency.

7   Spanish piety of Zumárraga's day was characterized by apparitions, pilgrimages to Marian shrines, and the exuberant devotional practices of the cult of the Virgin in Europe. Aztec religious ceremonies to Tonantzin were also characterized by pilgrimages, dramatic rituals with song and dance, as well as by solemn sacrifices. Fusion of the two was immediate and inevitable. Its development was nourished by the episcopate of the church. Robert Richard, *The Spiritual Conquest of Mexico: An Essay on the Apostolate and Evangelizing Methods of the Medicant Orders of New Spain: 1523-1572* (Berkeley: University of California Press, 1966), pp. 193ff; Jacque Lafaye, *Quetzalcoatl and Guadalupe: The Formation of the Mexican National Con sciousness 1531-1813,* trans. Benjamin Keen (Chicago: University of Chicago Press, 1976), Chap. 12.

8   Typical of the many feminist interpretations of Marian devotion as escapism are Marina Warner, *Alone of All Her Sex* (New York: Alfred Knopf, 1967), pp. xix-xxv; Simone de Beauvoir, *The Second Sex* (1952; rpt. New York: Random House Vintage

Book, 1974), p. 193ff; Mary Daly, *Beyond God the Father* (Boston: Beacon Press, 1973), pp. 84-86. Daly's works point to both the negative effects of Marian devotion and the possibilities of liberating interpretations. Sanchez (1648) and Elizondo (1983) would be representative of Latin American theologians who interpret Marian devotion as liberating.

9   Eric R. Wolfe, "The Virgin of Guadalupe: A Mexican National Symbol," *Journal of American Folklore*, Fall, 1958, pp. 34-39.

10   Miguel Sanchez' 1648 mms. developed a theological analogy between the Woman of Revelation and "The Image of the Virgin Mary, Mother of God, of Guadalupe. . ."

11   Sigüenza y Góngora, 17th century scholar, consciously linked the virtues and glories of Indian history to Guadalupan symbolism in what Lafaye called a march of the Creoles to spiritual emancipation from Spain; the poetry of Sor Juana Inez de la Cruz, Gongora's contemporary, also links Guadalupe to the Indian heritage and developing national consciousness of the Mexicans, applying the title, *Protectora Americana*, to the Virgin of Guadalupe a full century before the official proclamation. Lafaye, 59-75.

12   Jody Brant Smith, *The Image of Guadalupe* (Garden City, New York: Doubleday & Co., 1983). Smith provides a concise account of much of the significant research by artists, anthropologists, scientists, linguists, as well as his own ultra-violet photographic, spectroscopic and electron-microscopic studies made in 1978.

13   Eric R. Wolfe, pp. 34-39; Miguel Leon-Portilla (ed.), *Native Meso-American Spirituality* (New York: Paulist Press, 1980).

14   Francis Johnston, *The Wonder of Guadalupe: The Origin and Cult of the Miraculous Image of the Blessed Virgin in Mexico* (Rockford, Il.: Tan Books & Publishers, 1981) represents one of the most recent attempts to "prove" the supernatural character of the apparitions.

15   Wolfe, p. 38.

16   Patricia Green, "The 'Maguila' Women," *Nacla Report on the Americas*, XIV, No. 5 (1980), 14-19.

17   Octavio Paz, *The Labyrinth of Solitude: Life and Thought in Mexico* (1950), trans. Lysander Kemp (New York: Grove Press, 1961), p. 166.

18   Paz, p. 197.

19   Enrique Dussel, *Ethics and the Theology of Liberation* (New York: Orbis Books, 1978), pp. 55-59. For a more detailed explanation of Dussel's methodology, see his *History of the Church in Latin America* (Grand Rapids, Michigan: Eerdmans Publishing Co., 1981), pp. 1-19.

20   Dussel, *Ethics*, p. 118.

21   Clifford Geertz, *The Interpretation of Cultures* (New York: Basic Books, 1973), p. 90.

22   Andres Guererro, *The Significance of Nuestra Senora de Guadalupe and La Raza Cosmica in the Development of a Chicano Theology of Liberation* (Unpublished Ph.D. Dissertation, Harvard University, 1983), Chap. IV, p. 19.

23   Scholars concentrating on this task include Guererro; Elizondo; Thomas Ascheman, SVD, *Guadalupan Spirituality for Cross-Cultural Missionaries* (Master's thesis, Catholic Theological Union, Chicago, Il., 1983). Among Central and South American theologians dealing with popular religion see the works of Dussell, Galilea, Segundo, Scanoni, Bonini.

24   Rosemary Radford Ruether, *Sexism and God-Talk: Toward a Feminist Theology* (Boston: Beacon Press, 1983), p. 14.

25 Virgilio Elizondo, *Mary Prophetess and Model of Freedom for Responsibility* (San Antonio, Texas: Mexican American Cultural Center, n.d.).

26 Elizondo, *Mary*. . ., p. 4.

27 Elizondo, p. 1.

28 Elizondo, p. 1.

29 Elizondo, p. 10.

30 Raymond E. Brown, "Mary in the New Testament and in Catholic Life," *America* (May 15, 1982) pp. 374-379.

31 Brown, p. 379.

32 Brown, p. 379.

33 Gustavo Gutierrez, "Liberation, Theology, and Proclamation," *The Mystical and Political Dimension of the Christian Faith, Concilium* 96, (1974), pp. 57-77.

34 Sandra M. Schneiders, IHM, "Women in the Fourth Gospel and the Role of Women in the Contemporary Church," *Biblical Theology Bulletin* 12, (April 1982), p. 34.

35 Guererro, Chap. IV, p. 10.

36 Guererro, p. 23.

37 Guererro, Conclusion, p. 3.

38 Guererro, Chap. IV, pp. 11-14.

39 Ernesto Cardenal, *The Gospel of Solentiname I* (Maryknoll, New York: Orbis Books, 1976), pp. 16-18.

40 Cardenal, p. 20.

41 Cardenal, p. 25.

42 Cardenal, p. 28.

43 Cardenal, p. 31.

44 Rosemary Radford Ruether, *The Feminine Face of the Church* (Philadelphia: Westminster Press, 1977), pp. 32-33.

45 Rosemary Radford Ruether, "The Collision of History and Doctrine: The Brothers of Jesus and the Virginity of Mary," *Continuum* 7, No. 1 (Winter-Spring 1969), p. 104.

46 Ruether, *Feminine Face of the Church*, pp. 37-39.

47 Ruether, *Sexism and God-Talk*, pp. 152-158, 246; *Feminine Face of the Church*, p. 40.

48 Sandra Schneiders ("Women in the Fourth Gospel") claims that Mary's role is irrelevant for women because it is "either unique to her or universally significant for all Christians," p. 37; Elizabeth S. Fiorenza, "Feminist Theology as a Critical Theology of Liberation," *Woman: New Dimensions*, Walter Burkhardt, SJ (ed.) (New York: Paulist Press, 1977) states that "It can be questioned whether the myth (Mary-myth) can give to woman a new vision of equality and wholeness, since the myth almost never functioned as a symbol or justification of women's equality and leadership in church . . . and society, even though the myth contains elements which could have done so," p. 45, but points out that "Mary of Magdala was indeed a liberated woman," p. 48. Both Rosemary Ruether and the pre-post-Christian Mary Daly state similar opinions.

49 This is not to imply that Latin American feminist theologians cannot and may not be already be working to develop their own interpretations, but North American women cannot speak of the experiences of Mexican women although sexual violence in the United States does indicate that macho is not limited to Latin countries. See Mary Pellauer, "Violence Against Women: The Theological Dimension," *Christianity and Crisis* 43, No. 9 (May 30, 1983), pp. 206-212.

50 Fiorenza (*In Memory of Her*, p. 108) states that no Jewish feminist criticial recon-
    struction of first century Judaism has yet been done.
51 Fiorenza, p. 109
52 Brown, *Mary*, pp. 179-180
53 Brown, p. 101
54 Fiorenza, p. 132
55 Brown, pp. 150-151
56 Brown, pp. 191-192
57 Fiorenza, p. 141
58 For a summary of the traditions and theological arguments supporting Mary as
    mother of other children than Jesus, see R.R. Ruether, "The Collision of His-
    tory and Doctrine: The Brothers of Jesus and the Virginity of Mary," *Con-
    tinuum* 7, no. 1 (Winter-Spring 1969), pp. 93-104.
59 Fiorenza, p. 146: "That the saying (faithful discipleship) includes Mary, the mother
    of Jesus, among his faithful disciples, can only be derived from the Lukan redactional
    context (cf. Luke 2:19-51), not from the oldest tradition."
60 David Tracy, *The Analogical Imagination: Christian Theology and the Culture of
    Pluralism* (New York: Crossroads Publishing Co., 1981), pp. 407-411
61 Fiorenza's *In Memory of Her* represents her attempt to do just these things.

MARY IMMACULATE:
WOMAN OF FREEDOM,
PATRONESS OF THE
UNITED STATES
Carol Frances Jegen, BVM

When most people think of the Second Vatican Council, the first thing that comes to mind is rarely the person of Mary, although the council began on October 11, the feast of her maternity, in honor of the historic proclamation of *Theotokos,* Godbearer, at the Council of Ephesis in 431. Even for those persons who are aware of the significance of the date for the council's beginning and, even more important, are aware of the significance of the special chapter on Mary in *Lumen Gentium,* Vatican II's Dogmatic Constitution on the Church, little or no attention is paid to the dogma of the Immaculate Conception. At first glance, the council's emphasis on Mary in the midst of the church seems to be at the opposite pole from an emphasis on the Immaculate Conception—a truth of faith that appears to set Mary apart from the rest of us as "our tainted nature's solitary boast."[1]

The adult Catholic population in the United States is quite familiar with Mary as the Immaculate Conception. Statue after statue in our churches picture her as the woman crushing the serpent that symbolizes the power of original sin as interpreted from the Genesis story. Such statues and paintings also have been present in many Catholic homes. Most adult Catholics in our country can readily recall the aspiration, "O Mary, conceived without sin, pray for us who have recourse to thee." Some Catholics can still sing "Star-Crowned Virgin," a hymn proclaiming Mary as Patroness of the United States: "Hear our land's Magnificat. Hail, sweet Queen Immaculate." Through much planning and sacrifice on the part of Catholics throughout the United States, the National Shrine of the Immaculate Conception was built in Washington, D.C.[2] Long before, the French Jesuit explorer, Father Marquette, named the Mississippi River the river of Mary Immaculate. In a unique way, this gesture of devotion to the Immaculate Conception put the heartland of the United States, if not the whole country, under Mary's special protection.[3]

However, the familiarity of Catholics with Mary as the Immaculate Conception does not necessarily imply meaningful understanding of this article of faith. Clearly the dogma means Mary was uniquely blessed by God, graced from the very first moment of her existence. But this uniqueness of Mary is often interpreted by many Catholics as a separateness. Mary has too often been seen as significantly different from the rest of the human family. Many persons of sincere faith have interpreted her privileged position as an inherent incapability of understanding our human difficulties and struggles in any genuine experiential way. For too long Mary has been seen as one above and beyond us, rather than as one who shares with us a common experience as a Christian.

Almost imperceptibly, Vatican II's orientation on Mary, focusing on her oneness with us in the mystery of Christ and the church, began to challenge this mentality of apartness with respect to Mary.[4] The council implicitly called for a new understanding of the meaning of the Immaculate Conception. Indirectly, Vatican II raised a timely question regarding the meaning of this Marian dogma. How can the reality of the Immaculate Conception be seen by the faithful as a special blessing of God that not only brings Mary closer to us in human experience, but also gives the human family hope and direction for the future?

Historical Roots

Future directions in human life are rooted in past human experience. Future developments in a life of faith depend on previous stages of growth in the faith heritage of a community. Significant probings into the meaning of the Immaculate Conception for our times depend on some familiarity with the history of the church's faith life with respect to this Marian dogma. Thus far in the life of the church, no other revealed truth has had such a long controversial history.

Before considering some aspects of the history of the church's faith understanding that led to the dogmatic definition of the Immaculate Conception in 1854, it is helpful to distinguish between the question of the reality itself and the question of the reality's meaning in any historical period. The early theological study and discussion on Mary's Immaculate Conception focused more on reality than on meaning. That is to say, theologians such as Bernard of Clairvaux and Thomas Aquinas raised serious questions about the very existence of the Immaculate Conception.[5] Aquinas, particularly, focused on the difficulty of reconciling the universal redemption by Jesus with Mary's Immaculate Conception. Duns Scotus helped resolve that difficulty when he deftly demonstrated how the gift of the Immaculate Conception was merited by Jesus and given to Mary as one of the greatest of all redemptive acts. From this viewpoint, no one owes more to Jesus as Redeemer than Mary, the Immaculate one.

However, the theological question of Jesus as universal redeemer was not the only serious question in the minds of many Christians with respect to the reality of the Immaculate Conception. To this very day, many Protestant Christians have had great difficulties in believing this doctrine of faith because of the lack of explicit reference to the Immaculate Conception in scripture. The recent ecumenical scripture study, *Mary in the New Testament*, makes no reference to the Immaculate Conception in the very thorough exegesis of each New Testament text pertaining to the Mother of Jesus.[6]

Any comparison of contemporary scriptural interpretations with those from different historical periods must take into account recent advances in critical methodology. Today, we are very aware of the enormous difficulties in trying to recapture precise historical data from many scriptural texts. That is, contemporary scripture scholarship helps us read and hear and pray the scriptures in tune with the perspective of the community whose experience is captured somewhat in the sacred writings. We are much more cautious in 1983 about attributing historical facts to scriptural texts without sufficient evidence. This scholarly rigor at first sight might seem to impose stifling limitations on faith. On the contrary, such careful scripture scholarship helps put the role of the faith community in better perspective.

For example, recent discussions on the quest for the "historical Jesus" and the developing human consciousness of Jesus can be enlightening with respect to Mary. Any person familiar with history would find it difficult to deny the fact that Jesus and Mary really lived in a certain part of the world in a specific time. But no scripture scholar of any stature would claim that the New Testament gives us historical data about Jesus and his mother in the sense of a modern biography or a documentary. Consequently, while it is difficult to know exactly just what Jesus and Mary thought in many situations, it is not quite so difficult to grasp an overall picture of their way of life, their values, and their basic orientation to God.

Through the faith testimony of the primitive Christian community as recorded in the gospels, we do know much about Jesus of Nazareth and his mother, Mary. In those four gospels we also know that faith is a real life, capable of development in Christian history. In the New Testament and beyond, the quest of clarity of insight with respect to such maturing faith life moves us in the direction of theology. Recent scripture studies indicate how the gospel of John shows considerable theological development different from that of the gospel of Mark. Such theological development pertains to Mary as well as to Jesus and is pivotal in understanding how a dogma such as the Immaculate Conception is eventually defined as a revealed truth and officially proclaimed as such.[7]

The relation between maturing faith and theological development also helps pinpoint the problems involved in determining precise historical data. Small wonder that theological probings through the centuries have concentrated on constructing a rational argument that supports faith in the Immaculate Conception rather than on exploring the implications of this mystery.

Although some of the scriptural interpretations put forth in the past as ample evidence for Mary's Immaculate Conception could be challenged today, several points seem to be constant through centuries of exploration and interpretation. No matter what indications of this mystery may or may not be attributed strictly to the Genesis 3:15 text

("I will put enmity between you and the woman, and between your off-spring and hers; he will strike at your head, while you strike at his heel"), the symbolism of the woman/serpent imagery is paramount. Somehow this text, speaking of enmity between the serpent and the woman, has helped Christians interpret Immaculate Conception as an ultimate complete triumph over the power of evil, a culmination, as well as a foreshadowing, of the victorious life and death struggle in human experience.

Another key scriptural text that has received manifold interpretations related to the Immaculate Conception is the Lucan phrase often translated "full of grace" (Luke 1:28).[8] In the various translations and hermeneutical discussions of this text, along with the Genesis text, two insights predominate. First, Mary is specially favored by God because of her relation to Jesus. Second, Mary's unique giftedness gives her extra-ordinary power in the Christian community. Consequently, a tendency developed to exalt Mary's greatness in popular devotion, in art, and in theological thought. Significantly, in the devotional life of the people, the movement toward greater exaltation was coupled with an aware-ness of Mary's compassionate love as mother.[9]

Part of the history of the Christian community's developing faith in the Immaculate Conception can be traced in the liturgical life of the church. The feast of the Conception of Mary was celebrated in the East by the end of the seventh century[10] and in the West by the eleventh century.[11] In the fifteenth century, the feast was approved by Pope Sixtus IV.[12]

Early Christian writings also help trace a developing faith life in the mystery of the Immaculate Conception. Two examples are instructive. In the fifth century, St. Epiphanius wrote: "The immaculate sheep that brought forth Christ the Lamb of God was superior to all things, God alone excepted; she was more beautiful in her nature than the Cheru-bim, the Seraphim and the whole host of Angels. . . . Mary by grace was free from all stain of sin."[13] St. John Damascene testifies in the eighth century: "Our Lord preserved the soul, together with the body of the Blessed Virgin, in that purity which became her who was to receive a God in her womb; for as He is holy, He reposes only in holy places."[14]

In preparation for the dogmatic definition, when Pius IX gathered historical data from the universal church regarding the history of faith in Mary's Immaculate Conception, he accumulated overwhelming evidence. In his apostolic letter, *Ineffabilis Deus,* concerning the dogmatic definition of the Immaculate Conception, Pius IX alluded to the painstaking efforts undertaken by a special congregation of cardinals to "carefully weigh all those things which relate to the Immaculate Conception of the Virgin. . . ."[15]

The post-Vatican II church, in its efforts to become more truly universal in the embrace of various cultural expressions of faith, gives a certain urgency to the study of popular religiosity.[16] This seems to call for a phenomenological approach whereby new data of faith experience and expression can receive needed reverence and appreciation. Such study will inevitably focus on Marian devotion as it has matured through the Christian era. Perhaps the clues to the developing meaning of the Immaculate Conception lie there rather than exclusively in a strict scriptural exegesis.[17]

In the history of popular devotion to Mary, the Immaculate One, three women play very significant roles: St. Bridget of Sweden,[18] St. Catherine Labouré,[19] and St. Bernadette Soubirous.[20] Each of these women claimed Mary verified her Immaculate Conception in their prayer experiences. Particularly with respect to the world-renowned shrine at Lourdes, resulting from the appearances to Bernadette, and to Catherine Labouré's miraculous medal inscribed with the aspiration, "O Mary conceived without sin, pray for us who have recourse to thee," popular devotion to Mary took on new proportions.[21] Somehow, special faith experiences of three women—a princess, a sister, and a peasant— resonated in the hearts of countless Christians in all walks of life.

These particular prayer experiences of Bridget, Catherine, and Bernadette are classified as private revelations. Such experiences cannot be considered sources of faith, even though the church may judge such experiences authentic for the person involved. But in these particular cases historical records testify to responses by faith that greatly influenced devotion to Mary under the title Immaculate Conception.

Explicit faith witness to the Immaculate Conception is clearly part of the developing faith life of the Christian community. Faith in the Lord Jesus meant faith in the unique giftedness of his mother from the very beginning of her life. Long before the dogmatic definition of the Immaculate Conception in 1854, countless numbers of the Christian faithful knew in more simple terms what would be expressed in rather formal language.[22] "The Blessed Virgin Mary, at the first instant of her conception, by a singular privilege and grace of the Omnipotent God in virtue of the merits of Jesus Christ, the Saviour of mankind, was preserved immaculate from all stain of original sin. . . ."[23]

Because of the wording of the definition proclaiming the dogma of the Immaculate Conception, it is impossible to confront the question of meaning with regard to this Marian dogma and not face the difficult question of original sin. Perhaps no doctrine of Christian faith has had such a variety of interpretations and has caused as much pastoral confusion and anguish as the mystery of original sin. In contemporary times, Christian theologians have delved into the question once again, drawing on helpful insights from contemporary scripture scholarship, from new advances in philosophy, from recent discoveries in psychology and in the other social sciences, and from the findings of the natural sciences as well, insofar as the doctrine of original sin speaks to the whole cosmic order.

In a recent issue of *Theological Studies,* Brian McDermott summarized and discussed major recent theories on the meaning of the traditional doctrine of original sin.[24] Interestingly enough, this particular discussion makes no mention of the implications of any or all of these theological opinions as far as the Immaculate Conception is concerned. Perhaps it is precisely such theological study of the meaning of original sin in relation to Mary's Immaculate Conception that can give new insight into the many questions posed by these recent probings. So often in the history of theological thought one aspect of revealed truth is enlightened by another. Whatever else may be said about the mystery of original sin, it is only one aspect of the great mystery of our life in Jesus Christ. The Immaculate Conception is a part of that unfathomable mystery of human solidarity in Jesus Christ.[25] As such, the dogma of the Immaculate Conception can throw much-needed light on the difficult theological and pastoral question of the meaning of original sin.[26] This Marian dogma can also shift the focus of faith from a predominantly negative view of the human condition and potential to a new understanding of the transforming action of God in all of human life.

In his book *Mary, Mother of the Lord,* Karl Rahner explains how the dogma of the Immaculate Conception "indicates that the beginning of each spiritual being is important, and is laid down by God. God gives the beginning." Later he elaborates:

> For us too [God] eternally intended this saving grace from
> the beginning, in his eternity, even though it was only ef-
> fected in us after the beginning of our earthly, temporal life,
> in order that it might be plain that it is all [God's] grace,
> that nothing in our salvation belongs to us of ourselves.[27]

The eschatological significance of Mary's Immaculate Conception is one of the more helpful recent considerations.[28] If this doctrine is seen as essentially eschatological, that is, a mystery of final fulfillment in God's love, then in Mary we can see something of the fullness of our own salvation, of our ultimate union in God. Furthermore, we can know revitalized hope in the ongoing power of God's love operative in us now, overcoming the forces of evil and renewing the face of our earth.[29]

Focus on Freedom

In his article on recent theological reflection on the meaning of original sin, McDermott spoke of the need for Jesus the Redeemer to "transform the involuntary at the heart of freedom."[30] McDermott spoke of personal sin not just as a "product of my freedom but a mode of being of my freedom."[31] In such statements, this theologian strove to be faithful to the tradition that sees original sin as something intrinsic to the person and not exclusively a question of living in the situation of a sinful world, difficult and problematic as that might be. McDermott came to this conclusion after carefully assessing the current works of the major theologians who have attempted to give new insight into the mystery of original sin.[32]

In a subsequent article in *Chicago Studies,* McDermott clarified his thinking in the context of a liturgical experience of communal penance.[33] Pondering the two articles in complementary fashion, one can more readily understand McDermott's conclusion that the realization of personal sin in one's life brings the conviction that "I am, at root, not only free but also engaged in a subtle, pre-personal complicity with a power that only exists through my broken human freedom.[34] Conse-quently, in the experience of sincere confession, I bring the "root of my

sin," this "dark power within," to be liberated and healed.[35] The experience of personal sin throughout the history of the human family testifies to the mysterious deeper complicity within the human will that was
gradually named explicitly in the Christian tradition as the doctrine of
original sin.[35]

Relying somewhat on Paul Ricoeur, McDermott claimed three fundamental dimensions of sin: realism, solidarity, and power.[37] McDermott also referred to sin as power, dynamism, and captivity.[38] In such
contexts, he spoke of the power of Christ "who liberates what must be
liberated and pardons what needs to be pardoned."[39] This liberating
action of Jesus radically heals personal unfreedom, enabling one to
choose freely a life of love in God with ever greater directness, clarity,
and power.

Before pursuing the implications of this focus on freedom with respect to Mary's Immaculate Conception and its implications for us, it
will be helpful to mention briefly the thinking of other contemporary
theologians on the subjects of sin, grace, and freedom. The Latin American theologian, Juan Luis Segundo, in *Grace and the Human Condition,*
claimed "the starting point where grace finds us is not in a state of inno-
cence, but in a state of nonliberty." Segundo continued: "In making us
free through love, grace leads us toward the pole which, in its full totality, is God himself."[40] Segundo's phrase, "state of nonliberty," is conso-
nant with McDermott's "involuntary at the heart of freedom." When
Segundo spoke of our being made free through love, he also implied
that a dynamism is set at work that directs us Godward.

In Karl Rahner's discussion of the human condition in his book,
Grace in Freedom, he placed human freedom in the context of em-
powerment for the personal acceptance of God's self-gift.[41] Rahner said
freedom "is theological by its very nature, since in every free act God is
present, though not explicitly grasped, as its fundamental impulse and
final goal."[42] A bit later, Rahner reemphasized his concern to relate
human freedom with an immediacy to God. He asserted that "freedom
in its relation to its ground receives an immediacy to God through
which it becomes most radically the power to say Yes or No to God as
such."[43] Finally, Rahner insisted on the role of Jesus in setting freedom
free:

> God has made known in his Son the irrevocable decision

to set freedom free. Hence the history of freedom is salvation history. It is the experience realized in Jesus Christ that God has given himself to [human] freedom in what we call deifying grace in absolute nearness and as the ground of the free acceptance of this nearness. . . . This exercise of freedom in Christ is what St. Paul calls the "freedom of the children of God," the truly Christian freedom.[44]

The American theologian, Roger Haight, in his book, *The Experience and Language of Grace,* called his seventh chapter, "Liberation: A Contemporary Language of Graced Experience."[45] This theologian carefully traced key concepts of grace as developed throughout the Christian tradition. He too claimed "Human freedom is bound; . . . we cannot love God unless we experience the healing love of the God who first loves us."[46] Further, Haight said,". . . grace releases freedom from its inner constrictions and positively gives it a new horizon and scope, a new motive. . . . Quite simply grace is the force of God working in human existence moving it in love."[47]

In wrestling with these ideas of human unfreedom and nonliberty in relation to accepting God's love, and then in pondering our new freedom in Jesus, a freedom with its own inner dynamism for ever greater oneness with God who loves us intimately and without limit, we can turn now to Mary in the mystery of her Immaculate Conception. Mary shows us how a perfectly free person responds to God in love and corresponds with the inner dynamism of her human freedom as it enables her to reach out in love to all of God's creation. In Mary we see most clearly what our own life of love in God is capable of becoming, because the same powerful freeing action of Jesus is operative in us.

Such a life of love in God necessarily involves a communing with God, or "dialogical" experience. All love demands communing in ever greater intensity. Alszeghy and Flick, two European theologians, have focused much of their extensive study of the doctrine of original sin on the reality of dialogical alienation from God, and consequently, from human persons.[48] Relying heavily on personalist philosophy, with its concerns for personal development, these theologians concentrated on the impossibility of a person "subject to sin's power to hear and effectively respond to God's summons, voiced through creation, to become a son or daughter of the Father."[49]

In relating this contemporary theologizing on the meaning of original sin to the dogma of the Immaculate Conception, a Spanish theologian, Cascante Dávila, in singling out the positive dynamic aspect of this dialogical emphasis, confirmed my own conviction that one way to discover greater understanding of Mary's giftedness is to ponder seriously her dialogical relation with God.[50] This particular focus seems a most promising one to pursue for two reasons. First, its positive emphasis on personal dialog concentrates on the relation of freedom to a life of love; second, a consideration of personal dialog in Mary's regard brings us to those key scriptural texts on the Mother of Jesus. If there is ongoing difference of opinion about the direct scriptural evidence for the Immaculate Conception, there seems to be unanimous agreement on the part of contemporary scripture scholars on the significance of the Synoptic text referring to Mary's "hearing the word of God" (Luke 8:19-21).[51]

In the light of these recent theological developments, perhaps one of the most helpful ways to gain new insight into the meaning of the Immaculate Conception and its relevance for all of us is to ponder prayerfully those scriptural texts that point directly to Mary's dialogical relation to God. Those scriptural scenes highlighting Mary's prayerfulness help us see what is most basic in her life as disciple, as one most closely united with Jesus. Those scriptural passages show us the power and artistry of redemptive love tracing a pattern of ongoing dialog, of listening and responding, of questioning and pondering in uninhibited freedom.

Before considering further any other specific gospel texts, it is important to emphasize the first picture of Mary in the primitive church as portrayed in the book of Acts. Mary is singled out by name in that first Christian community gathered in prayerful preparation for the coming of the Holy Spirit (Acts 1:14). This experience of the early church praying with Mary must have had considerable influence on the gospel writers, particularly on the Lucan author. He not only emphasizes how Mary, as perfect disciple, "heard the word" (Luke 8:19), but also accents her prayerfulness in the infancy narrative. "Mary treasured all these things and reflected on them in her heart" (Luke 2:19). "His mother meanwhile kept all these things in her memory" (Luke 2:51).[52]

Helpful as these texts might be in portraying Mary as a prayerful woman, enjoying a familial relation with God, the great Marian prayer text in scripture is the Magnificat (Luke 1:46-55). There we encounter the fruitfulness of Mary's dialog with God as her joy-filled spirit proclaims the greatness, the holiness, the mercy of God for all ages. Pouring forth from a heart given to God in total perfect freedom, the Magnificat resonates with those persons in every generation whose hearts yearn for freedom from oppression of all kinds. Rightly could the Magnificat be called a canticle of freedom.

As a canticle of freedom, the Magnificat is our song as well as Mary's. There is a dynamic movement in this prayer characteristic of the freeing power inherent in any loving dialog. Any genuine communing in love always strengthens and frees the love relationship for more beautiful expressions within and beyond itself. In the Magnificat, a heart perfectly free from any kind of self-centeredness reaches out to extend such freedom to others, confident that the same redeeming power of God will continue to free the rich and the hungry, the lowly and the mighty, for greater enjoyment of God's own life of love.

Mary Immaculate, Patroness of the United States

With this note of freedom, let us consider briefly Mary's significance in our lives as citizens of the United States of America. Although several other pertinent questions regarding traditional explanations of the meaning of original sin are raised by contemporary theologians, the question of human freedom seems to lend greatest intelligibility to the meaning of the Immaculate Conception in our times. In theological circles, a focus on freedom echoes immediately with the notion of liberation as developed by Latin American theologians.[58] But in the United States of America, a country dedicated to the ideals of liberty and justice for all, there is a particular attraction to the exploration of authentic human freedom. Understanding the Immaculate Conception in relation to human freedom becomes even more pertinent to American Catholics in the light of Mary Immaculate as Patroness of the United States.

However, when we consider human freedom within the context of the United States heritage, the focus is usually on political understandings, not so directly on the personal freedom at the very core of human existence.[54] Fortunately, today several scholars are becoming aware of the intrinsic relation between the lack of interior freedom on a personal level and the lack of social and political structures that can provide and maintain freedom from oppression in the civic order.[55]

Social and political structures are created by human beings. As such, these structures are designed and sustained through a series of often complex free choices. Recent theological probings by writers such as Sobrino, Boff, Hollenbach, and Haight often are focused on situations of societal injustice. In the writings of such theologians and others, unjust structures are termed sinful, needing to be freed through systemic change.[56] Roger Haight, in making careful and needed distinctions and comparisons between personal sin and social sin, commented:

> . . . because the social systems or institutions by which human affairs are structured are not part of nature but functions of human freedom and able to be changed, insofar as they victimize, oppress or are generally harmful and damaging to persons, they are sinful at least in an objective or material sense.[57]

Past understandings of original sin, continuing in current pastoral orientations, have had an unfortunate impact on this whole area of social structures and political systems. A one-sided stress on the all-pervasive aspect of original sin in human life has engendered a lack of hope in many religious people concerning any genuine transformation of societal structures.[58] Far too many Christians have been convinced that the redemptive action of Jesus pertains exclusively to individual lives. Salvation, like religion, is considered a very individual matter. Such a self-centered religious mentality holds that personal transformation is all that can be expected this side of eternity.[59] In sharp contrast, developing social teaching of the church has done much to illustrate that a religious mentality unconcerned about transforming social structures is not in tune with the gospel of Jesus.[60] The Synod of 1971 in its historic document, *Justice in the World,* clearly proclaimed:

> Action on behalf of justice and participation in the transformation of the world fully appear to us as a constitutive dimension of the preaching of the gospel, or, in other words, of the church's mission for the redemption of the

human race and its liberation from every oppressive situation (6).[61]

In 1846, when the Sixth Council of Baltimore decreed that the Blessed Virgin Mary, under the title of Immaculate Conception, was Patroness of the Church in the United States,[62] the religious emphasis and language in that statement were obviously that of the nineteenth century. The Decree of 1846 stated:

> By the aid of her prayers, we entertain the confident hope that we will be strengthened to perform the arduous duties of our ministry, and that you will be enabled to practice the sublime virtues of which her life presents a most perfect example.[63]

Surely, no devout Catholic would minimize the importance of Mary's help in the "arduous duties of ministry" and in the practice of the "sublime virtues." In fairness, it is important to remember the contextual climate of religious understanding was conducive to emphasizing personal sanctity, often to the exclusion of societal involvement.

A pastoral letter of the bishops of the United States issued in 1919 reflected this religious mentality in more specific terms.

> But if all generations should call her blessed, and if the peoples of earth should glory in her protection, we in the United States have a particular duty to honor Mary Immaculate as the heavenly Patroness of our country. Let her Blessed influence preserve our Catholic homes from all contagion of evil, and keep our children in pureness of heart. Let us also pay her the tribute of public honor in a way that will lead all our people to a fuller appreciation of Mary, the perfect woman and the surpassing model of motherhood.[64]

In the light of these church teachings from the past, well might we question the meaning of the symbolism so frequently associated with artistic portrayals of Mary Immaculate—the woman crushing the head of the serpent. The ultimate triumph over the power of evil represented in such artwork was usually related to salvation in very personal terms. Without losing the validity of such symbolic interpretation, can we now relate the redemptive power of this symbolism to the societal order? Can the Immaculate Conception truly become an eschatological symbol for us, calling us forth in confident hope in our societal struggle for the freedom necessary for justice and peace? Can the Immaculate Conception be our symbol of human freedom from the power of evil wherever it exists? Can the Immaculate Conception become a vital symbol of the power of God's love, freely accepted and operative in our lives?

If Mary Immaculate, Patroness of the United States, is to become a viable symbol for us in our ongoing struggle for freedom from oppression, and above all, in our current global struggle for freedom from the demonic evil of war, then our pastoral ministers and religious educators must rise to an urgent and inspiring educational challenge. New meanings for this symbol must be interiorized and made operative in the minds and hearts of our people of faith, young and old.

As we truly face our time in history as a new moment for peace and for justice, we must also face in a realistic manner the human suffering that continues to be a part of the struggle for the freedom essential for authentic justice and genuine peace. Here, too, the woman/serpent symbolism has much to say to us. For some time, scripture scholars have reminded us about sound exegesis of the Genesis text, "I will put enmity between you and the woman, and between your offspring and hers; He will strike at your head, while you strike at his heel" (Genesis 3:15).[65] This text includes the notion of constant hostility and threat of harm on the part of both adversaries.[66] Clearly in the life of Mary and her son, Jesus, together with countless persons who have been interiorly free enough to enter into the struggle for justice and for peace, untold suffering was and often is a part of their lives. How readily we can refer to Mary, woman of freedom, strengthening us to enter freely into such struggle and suffering with undaunted faith in the ongoing presence of her risen son, with vibrant hope in the eventual triumph of good over evil, with forgiving and even joyful love able to transform our enemies into friends.

However, we must avoid any tendency to exalt Mary above and beyond our common human experience of faith-filled lives. That is, we must let Mary be in our midst in a realistic way. We must believe in and experience the power of her person actively engaged in all our struggles for freedom, whether those struggles be within the depths of our personal lives or in our common endeavors for freedom from any and all forms of societal oppression. Vatican II's document on *The Church in the Modern World* proclaimed "authentic freedom is an exceptional sign of the divine image within the human person" (GS 17).[67] How important it is to realize that such a claim is made for every human person. In Mary we see what authentic human freedom means. In Mary we see the undaunted power of a woman, totally free in her love for God and for God's entire human family. In Mary we see what we are called to become as free persons.

In 1973, when U.S. bishops wrote their pastoral letter on Mary,[68] in several ways they emphasized Mary's oneness with us in the mystery of the church. This letter speaks of Mary's influence in overcoming the evils of "the succession of wars that grow in horror as technology improves, the oppression of underprivileged people at home and abroad, the imbalance between rich and poor countries. . . ."[69] Some of the bishops' remarks referred explicitly to the mystery of the Immaculate Conception. The letter stated:

> Of ecumenical import also are Catholic efforts to show that such beliefs about the Mother of the Lord as her initial freedom from original sin (the Immaculate Conception) and her final union with the risen Christ (the Assumption) are not isolated privileges, but mysteries filled with meaning for the whole church (102).

> What the church has said about the effects of redemption in Mary, she has affirmed in other ways and at other times of us all. The Immaculate Conception and the Assumption, as we sought to show earlier in this letter, are basically affirmations about the nature of human salvation (111).

One of the most basic "effects of redemption in Mary" is a prayerfulness attuned to the unredeemed aspects of life. Mary's continuing dialog with God is the primary expression of her inner freedom. This prayerful dialog directly with God frees Mary for honest dialog with other persons, illustrated in the Cana story, a dialog so essential for furthering human community and thereby establishing a just and peaceful world.[70] In 1854 when the dogma of the Immaculate Conception was proclaimed, Mary was affirmed as one who was "always conversant with God."[71] In 1974, when Paul VI wrote *Marialis Cultus,* he referred to Mary as one "taken into dialog with God," giving her "active and responsible consent" to that "event of world importance," the Incarnation. How significant that the context of this passage, relating Mary's prayer to responsible societal action, is an invitation to contemplation of Mary extended to the "modern woman, anxious to participate with decision-making power in the affairs of the community" (37).[72]

Like Mary, continuing loving dialog with God must be our primary expression of inner freedom also. In prayer we gain the freedom and strength and courage to enter into honest loving dialog with one another, really to "[speak] the truth in love" (Ephesians 4:15). Therein lies the key to any effective struggle against evil. In the final analysis, only God's love freely operative in us can overcome the power of darkness.[73]

Footnotes

1 William Wordsworth, "The Virgin," *The Poetical Works of William Wordsworth,* (ed.) E. Deselincourt and Helen Darbishire (Oxford: Clarendon Press, 1963), p. 373

2 In the pastoral letter of the bishops of the United States issued in 1919, the statement was made, "But if all generations should call her blessed, and if the peoples of earth should glory in her protection, we in the United States have a particular duty to honor Mary Immaculate as the heavenly patroness of our country. . . . As Pope Benedict has declared, it is eminently fitting that the devotion of American Catholics to the Mother of God should find expression in a temple worthy of our Celestial Patroness." Quoted in Bernard McKenna, *The Dogma of the Immaculate Conception* (Washington, D.C., 1929), p. 522. Bishop Thomas J. Shahan, fourth rector of the Catholic University of America, is credited with the suggestion of building the national shrine of the Immaculate Conception. See U.S. Catholic Bishops, *Behold Your Mother: Woman of Faith* (Washington, D.C.: United States Catholic Conference, 1973), p. 55.

3 In 1673 the Mississippi River was called the River of the Immaculate Conception, *ibid.,* p. 53; McKenna, *The Dogma of the Immaculate Conception,* p. 529.

4 Otto Semmelroth, "Commentary on *Lumen Gentium,* Chapter VIII," in Herbert Vorgrimler (ed.), *Commentary on the Documents of Vatican II* (West Germany: Herder and Herder, 1967), p. 287, #53

5 Carlo Balic, "The Medieval Controversy over the Immaculate Conception up to the Death of Scotus," in Edward D. O'Connor (ed.), *The Dogma of the Immaculate Conception* (Notre Dame, Indiana: University of Notre Dame Press, 1958), p. 161f. Also see Bernard McKenna, *The Dogma of the Immaculate Conception,* Ch. VI, "St. Thomas and the Immaculate Conception," and Ch. XIX, "St. Bernard and the Immaculate Conception."

6 Raymond E. Brown, *et. al.* (eds.), *Mary in the New Testament* (Philadelphia: Fort-

ress Press and New York: Paulist Press, 1978). A brief complementary study coming from Latin America is that of Horacio Bojorge, *The Image of Mary,* trans. Aloysius Owen (Staten Island: Alba House, 1977).

7   A significant observtion on this point was made by Cardinal Newman. "Let me take the doctrine which Protestants consider our greatest difficulty, that of the Immaculate Conception . . . it is a simple fact to say, that Catholics have not come to believe it because it is defined, but that it was defined because they believed it." J.H. Newman, *Apologia Pro Vita Sua* (London, 1865), Part VII, pp. 278-279 (in later editions, Ch. V) as quoted in O'Connor, *The Dogma of the Immaculate Conception,* p. 17.

8   Christopher O'Donnell, *Life in the Spirit and Mary* (Wilmington: Michael Glazier, 1981), p. 29. An interesting observation is made with respect to Protestant theology's emphasis on "grace alone" and the Catholic belief in the Immaculate Conception, an absolutely gratuitous gift of God.

9   Owen F. Cummings, "Understanding the Immaculate Conception," *Furrow* 30 (December, 1979), pp. 767-771, esp. p. 768

10 Richard P. McBrien, *Catholicism* (Minneapolis: Winston Press, 1981), p. 873

11 *Ibid.*

12 *Ibid.,* p. 879

13 Peter Brookby (ed.), *Virgin Wholly Marvelous* (Cambridge: Ravengate Press, 1981), p. 46

14 *Ibid.,* p. 47

15 Pius IX, *Ineffabilis Deus,* as quoted in McKenna, *The Dogma of the Immaculate Conception,* p. 19

16 Two recent documents concerned with Hispanic peoples point to the need for appreciating popular expressions of faith. See John Eagleson and Philip Scharper (eds.), *Puebla and Beyond* (Maryknoll: Orbis, 1979), pp. 184-188; Hispanic Bishops of the United States, *The Bishops Speak with the Virgin* (Maryknoll: Revista, 1981), pp. 6, 7, 21-23.

17 Hilda Graef, *Mary, a History of Doctrine and Devotion,* Vol. II (New York: Sheed and Ward, 1965), pp. 78-83

18 McBrien, *Catholicism,* p. 877. Also see Johannes Jørgensen, *Saint Bridget of Sweden,* Vol. II, trans. Ingeborg Lund (London: Longmans Green, 1954). Bridget reports Mary's testimony in the following words: "The truth is this, that I was conceived without sin. . . . That hour, therefore, in which I was conceived, may well be called a golden hour, for then began the salvation of mankind, and darkness gave way to light" (p. 257).

19 O'Connor, *The Dogma of the Immaculate Conception,* p. 472; McBrien, *Catholicism,* p. 879; Graef, *Mary, a History of Doctrine and Devotion,* pp. 85-87

20 McKenna, *The Dogma of the Immaculate Conception,* p. 157f; McBrien, *Catholicism,* p. 880

21 Graef, *Mary, a History of Doctrine and Devotion.* Graef remarked: "The tremendous popularity of the Medal, to which soon numerous miracles were attributed, had also a great influence on the definition of the Immaculate Conception, as it impressed the doctrine on the consciousness of Catholic people and led to a growing demand to have it solemnly defined" (p. 87).

22 Cummings, *Understanding the Immaculate Conception,* p. 770

23 Piux IX, *Ineffabilis Deus,* as quoted in McKenna, p. 21. The original Latin wording, given on pp. 222-223, is: ". . . declaramus pronunciamus et definimus, doctrinam,

quae tenet beatissimam Virginem Mariam in primo instanti suae Conceptionis fuisse singulari omnipotentis Dei gratia et privilegio, intuitu meritorum Christi Jesu Salvatoris humani generis, ab omni originalis culpae labe praeservatam immunem, esse a Deo revelatam, atque idcirco ab omnibus fidelibus firmiter constanterque credendam."

24 Brian McDermott, "The Theology of Original Sin: Recent Developments," *Theological Studies* 38:3 (Sept., 1977), 478-512. In this comprehensive article McDermott treated the following theologians: Karl-Heinz Weger, Karl Rahner, Charles Baumgartner, Maurizio Flick and Zoltan Alszeghy, Sharon MacIsaac, Karl Schmitz-Moorman, Juan Luis Segundo, Domiciano Fernandez, and G. Vandervelde, who in turn discussed, in addition, Schoonenberg, Vanneste, and Bauman. In his summary remarks McDermott also referred to Paul Ricoeur.

25 Karl Rahner, *Theological Investigations*, Vol. I (Baltimore: Helicon, 1965). In his sixth chapter, "The Immaculate Conception," Rahner emphasized the importance of seeing how a "particular truth fits into the whole of Christian faith, how it derives its life from this whole and how its meaning and content can be clarified by reference to the whole" (p. 202). Michael Meilach's recent study, *Mary Immaculate in the Divine Plan* (Wilmington: Michael Glazier, 1981), sheds interesting light on the Immaculate Conception in the context of the whole creative process.

26 Joaquin Maria Alonso, "Questiones Actuales: IV ¿Desmitologización del dogma de la Inmaculada Concepción de Maria?" *Ephemerides Mariologicae* 23 (1973). In his concluding remarks the author stressed that new understandings of original sin must be in harmony with the church's faith in the Immaculate Conception.

27 Karl Rahner, *Mary, Mother of the Lord* (New York: Herder and Herder, 1963), pp. 44, 49. Also see Cyril Vollert, *A Theology of Mary* (New York: Herder and Herder, 1965), p. 207

28 Cummings, "Understanding the Immaculate Conception," p. 770. Also see Wolfgang Beinert, "Marian Devotion: A Pastoral Opportunity," *Theology Digest* 29:2 (Summer, 1981). Beinert asserted: "As paradigm, Mary is also symbol or sacrament of the church's hope. In her, the church has irrevocably attained its goal. Mary means that God is true to his promises" (p. 157).

29 In his article on "The Immaculate Conception" in *Theological Investigations, op. cit.,* Karl Rahner claimed that without Mary's Immaculate Conception it is "impossible to think of Redemption as victorious" (p. 213). Also see J. Juan Diaz Vilar, *Miriam la Mujer Galilea* (New York: Northeast Catholic Pastoral Center for Hispanics, 1982). Vilar stated, "The Immaculate Conception is the hope of us all that one day, with Mary, we shall experience ourselves fully cleansed and totally filled with the love of God" (p. 101).

30 McDermott, "The Theology of Original Sin: Recent Developments," p. 511

31 *Ibid.,* p. 511

32 For a list of the theologians considered, see note 24 of this chapter.

33 Brian McDermott, "From Symbol to Doctrine: Creation and Original Sin," *Chicago Studies*, 19:1 (Spring, 1980), 35-50

34 *Ibid.,* p. 46

35 *Ibid.,* p. 49

36 *Ibid.*

37 McDermott, "The Theology of Original Sin: Recent Developments," p. 511

38 McDermott, "From Symbol to Doctrine: Creation and Original Sin," p. 49

39 McDermott, "The Theology of Original Sin: Recent Developments," p. 510

40   Juan Luis Segundo, *Grace and the Human Condition*, trans. John Drury (Maryknoll: Orbis, 1973), p. 46
41   Karl Rahner, *Grace in Freedom*, trans. and adapted Hilda Graef (New York: Herder and Herder, 1969)
42   *Ibid.*, p. 206
43   *Ibid.*, p. 210. Also see George Dyer, "The Need for Salvation: A Pastoral Perspective," *Chicago Studies* 21:3 (Fall, 1982), pp. 293-306, esp. p. 302
44   Rahner, *Grace in Freedom*, p. 224
45   Roger Haight, *The Experience and Language of Grace* (New York: Paulist, 1979)
46   *Ibid.*, p. 152
47   *Ibid.*, p. 157
48   Zoltan Alszeghy and Maurizio Flick, "A Personalistic View of Original Sin," *Theology Digest* 15:3 (Autumn, 1967), pp. 190-196; Zoltan Alszeghy and Maurizio Flick, "An Evolutionary View of Original Sin," *Theology Digest* 15:3 (Autumn, 1967), pp. 197-202. For Brian McDermott's discussion of Alszeghy and Flick, see "The Theology of Original Sin: Recent Developments," p. 488f.
49   McDermott, "The Theology of Original Sin: Recent Developments," p. 489
50   Juan M. Cascante Dávila, "El Dogma de la Inmaculada en las Nuevas Interpretaciones Sobre el Pecado Original," *Estudios Marianos* XLII (Barcelona, 1978), pp. 115-146, esp. p. 138
51   Raymond Brown, *Mary in the New Testament*, p. 167f. Also see Eamon Carroll, *Understanding the Mother of Jesus* (Wilmington: Michael Glazier, 1979), p. 15f
52   *Ibid.*, p. 147f
53   Gustavo Gutierrez, Leonardo Boff, Jon Sobrino, etc.
54   Karl Rahner, *Grace in Freedom*, p. 204
55   A most helpful article in this regard is Richard Roach's "Tridentine Justification and Justice" in *The Faith That Does Justice*, (ed.) John C. Haughey (New York: Paulist, 1977), pp. 181-206
56   Strong statements in this regard are found in the *Puebla Documents*, #1154 and #1155. See Philip Scharper and John Eagleson (eds.), *Puebla and Beyond*. Also see Antonio Moser, "Sin as Negation of the Kingdom," *Theology Digest* 30:1 (Spring, 1982), pp. 27-30
57   Roger Haight, *The Experience and Language of Grace*, p. 173
58   Brian McDermott, "From Symbol to Doctrine: Creation and Original Sin," p. 42
59   Richard Roach, "Tridentine Justification and Justice," p. 195f
60   See Joseph Gremillion, *The Gospel of Peace and Justice* (Maryknoll: Orbis, 1976)
61   *Ibid.*, p. 514
62   Bernard McKenna, *The Dogma of the Immaculate Conception*, p. 517. Also see U.S. Catholic Bishops, *Behold Your Mother: Woman of Faith*, p. 53f
63   Bernard McKenna, *The Dogma of the Immaculate Conception*, p. 518
64   *Ibid.*, p. 522
65   *New American Bible* translation
66   A.M. Dubarle, *The Biblical Doctrine of Original Sin*, trans. E.M. Stewart (New York: Herder and Herder, 1964), p. 77. For an overview on the question of sin in the Old Testament, see Alphonse Spilly, "Sin and Alienation in the Old Testament: The Personalist Approach," *Chicago Studies* 21:3 (Fall, 1982), pp. 211-226
67   As quoted in Joseph Gremillion, *The Gospel of Peace and Justice*, p. 256
68   In the "Introduction," #11, special mention is made of the fact that this letter was

written in the Holy Year 1973. It seems a happy coincidence that this present study of Mary is undertaken during another Holy Year, 1983

69   U.S. Catholic Bishops, *Behold Your Mother: Woman of Faith*, p. 51

70   José García Murga, "Maria en Tiempos de Libertad y Liberacion," *Ephemerides Marilogicae* 29 (1979), pp. 207-221

71   Bernard McKenna, *The Dogma of the Immaculate Conception*, p. 15

72   Paul VI, *Marialis Cultus* (Washington: United States Catholic Conference, 1974), p. 27

73   Segundo Galilea, *Following Jesus*, trans. Sr. Helen Philipps (Maryknoll: Orbis, 1981), p. 49; Jurgen Moltman, *The Trinity and the Kingdom of God*, trans. Margaret Kohl (San Francisco: Harper and Row, 1981), esp. pp. 216-222. Moltman's development of the Trinitarian aspects of human freedom has special significance for our understanding of Mary. Although Moltman did not point to such implications, his work has interesting implications for Mariology